Atherton Tablelands Tourism, Queensland Australia

Travel Guide

Author
David Mills.

SONITTEC PUBLISHING. All rights reserved. No part of this publication may be reproduced, distributed, or transmitted in any form or by any means, including photocopying, recording, or other electronic or mechanical methods, without the prior written permission of the publisher, except in the case of brief quotations embodied in critical reviews and certain other noncommercial uses permitted by copyright law. For permission requests, write to the publisher, addressed "Attention: Permissions Coordinator," at the address below.

Copyright © 2019 Sonittec Publishing
All Rights Reserved

First Printed: 2019.

Publisher:
SONITTEC LTD
College House, 2nd Floor
17 King Edwards Road,
Ruislip
London
HA4 7AE.

Table of Content

SUMMARY 1
ABOUT ATHERTON TABLELANDS 4
   DESTINATIONS.. 9
      Atherton 9
         Celebrating Chocolate...................................... 12
         Atherton Tablelands Wonders That Will Take Your Breath Away 17
         Mountain Lakes. Barrine & Eacham..................... 25
      Chillagoe to Mutchilba 28
      Kuranda 32
      Herberton & Irvinebank 35
      Malanda.. 38
      Mareeba 41
      Millaa Millaa 46
      Mount Molloy to Julatten................................... 50
      Ravenshoe to Mount Garnett............................. 53
      Tinaroo 59
      Tolga & Walkamin 61
      Yungaburra & Crater Lakes................................ 63
   ACTIVITIES, SIGHTS AND TOUR.. 68
      Four-wheel Drive Adventures Beyond Mareeba 69
      Free diving Lake Eacham 72
      Atherton Tablelands has full spread of events................ 74
      Lake Barrine... 79
      Geological-Wonders... 81
      Hiking and Walking 85
         Short Walks.. 85
         5 Awesome Spring Hiking Adventures 87
         Top Spots: Lookouts to Look For........................ 90
         World War 2 Trail... 94
      Birding and Wildlife 98
      Touring 101
      National Parks Guide 104
      Ancien Rainforest 107

Getting Here 111
Lake Tinaroo 113
Crater Lakes 114
Yunga Burra 118
Malanda 122
Millaa Millaa 124
Atherton 127
Herberton and Irvinebank 132
Kuranda 136
Tolga and Walkamin 143
Chillagoe and Petford 147
Savannah Way 149
Cassowary Coast 156
FOOD AND DRINK 165
Your Guide to Atherton Tablelands' Wineries 165
Experience the Atherton Tablelands Craft Distilleries and Wineries 169
5 Cute and Quirky Eats on the Atherton Tablelands 174
Yungaburra Christmas Markets 177
The Atherton Tablelands On a Plate 178

Atherton Tablelands Tourism, Queensland Australia

Summary

The world is a book and those who do not travel read only one page.

It is indeed very unfortunate that some people feel traveling is a sheer waste of time, energy and money. Some also find traveling an extremely boring activity. Nevertheless, a good majority of people across the world prefer traveling, rather than staying inside the confined spaces of their homes. They love to explore new places, meet new people, and see things that they would not find in their homelands. It is this very popular attitude that has made tourism, one of the most profitable, commercial sectors in the world.

People travel for various reasons. Some travel for work, others for fun, and some for finding mental peace. Though every person may have his/her own reason to go on a journey, it is essential to note that traveling, in itself, has some inherent advantages. For one, for some days getting away from everyday routine is a pleasant change. It not only refreshes one's body, but also mind and soul. Traveling to a distant place and doing exciting things that are not thought of otherwise, can rejuvenate a person, who then returns home, ready to take on new and more difficult challenges in life and work. It makes a person forget his worries, problems, frustrations, and fears, albeit for some time. It gives him a chance to think wisely and constructively. Traveling also helps to heal; it can mend a broken heart.

For many people, traveling is a way to attain knowledge, and perhaps, a quest to find answers to their questions. For this, many people prefer to go to faraway and isolated places. For believers, it is a search for God and to gain higher knowledge; for others, it is a search for inner peace. They might or might not find what they are looking for, but such an experience certainly enriches their lives

David Mills

About Atherton Tablelands

The Atherton Tablelands is the name given to the rich agricultural lands inland from Cairns. It is home to a number of towns like Kuranda, Ravenshoe and Atherton. Right troughout the region are many tourist attractions such as lake Eacham, the Curtain Fig tree and the Undarra Lava Tubes. From Cairns to Kuranda, the road winds up the mountain with views of the coast and rainforest. Upon arrival you will discover the quaint little township of Kuranda with country style markets and galleries. The Australian Butterfly Sanctuary is brilliant and the walk through free flight aviary of Birdworld, where birds live freely is a wonderful experience. You will discover lots to do in Kuranda and accommodation ranges from caravan parks to bed & breakfasts.

The tropical hinterland and tablelands are a must see when visiting far north Queensland. One of the most popular attractions are the Crystal Caves. Take a short drive up to Hallorans Hill for a dramatic scenic lookout over Lake Tinaroo and the rolling hillside that surrounds Atherton. A day spent driving around the Atherton tablelands area and having a picnic lunch, will be one of your holiday highlights.

Region Overview

The Atherton Tablelands is a diverse region, covering an area of 64,768 square kilometres and home to 45,243 people (estimated resident population, Census 2011). The main population centres on the Atherton Tablelands are Mareeba and Atherton.

Smaller towns include Malanda, Herberton, Kuranda, Ravenshoe, Millaa Millaa, Chillagoe, Dimbulah, Mt Garnet, Mt Molloy, Tinaroo and Yungaburra.

The region spreads westwards and southwards from the coastal escarpment behind Cairns and incorporates parts of the Wet Tropics World Heritage Area to the east, the Einasleigh Uplands to the south, the Gulf Plains to the west and the Cape York Peninsula bioregion to the north.

The mountainous region in the east reaches heights above 1600 metres, including Queensland's highest mountain Mt Bartle Frere at 1622 metres.

Because of its altitude, the region does not suffer from temperature extremes or the high humidity experienced in coastal areas. The northern part of the region enjoys cool, dry winters and warm, wet summers with minimum daily temperatures in winter rarely falling below 15ºC and maximum daily summer temperatures rarely exceeding 35ºC. To the south, rainfall is much higher with the area around Topaz recording some of the highest annual rainfall in Australia. Temperatures are also lower with a range of between 17 and 25ºC from September to June and between 5 and 14ºC from July to August.

The considerable range in elevation, rainfall and soil types has produced an incredibly diverse and beautiful region. There is a prolific diversity in natural flora and fauna, ranging from tropical highland rainforests to dry tropical savannah.

Water, soils and diverse growing conditions have supported development of a wide range of agricultural and horticultural cropping operations. The region's farmers and support services represent, in most cases, best international practice in farming in a tropical environment.

Water supplied from Tinaroo Dam enables a tremendous range of fruit and vegetables to be grown to supply both the domestic and overseas markets.

The range of crops grown is truly amazing and includes avocados, bananas, cashews, citrus, coffee, cow pea, custard apples, dolichos, flowers, fresh herbs, grapes, grass seed, legume seed, lettuce, longans, lychees, macadamia, maize, mangoes, mixed vegetables, navy beans, potatoes, passionfruit, papaya, peaches, peanuts, pineapples, pumpkins, sorghum, sugar cane, sweet potatoes, tea tree, tomatoes, native trees, turf and watermelons.

The cattle industry also plays a significant role in the region's economy and in recent years the value of animals produced in the region has been approximately $35 million per annum.

To the south, around the Malanda/Millaa Millaa area, the dairy industry is significant and the Atherton Tablelands dairy industry is the only tropical dairy industry in Australia and one of the few globally. Other agriculture based industries include poultry, fruit wineries, aquaculture and timber.

Destinations

Atherton

The bustling township of Atherton is 95 km south-west from Cairns, travelling via the Kuranda Range. Atherton is on the Kennedy Highway and the town centre includes a comprehensive shopping centre, showgrounds, hospital and Olympic size swimming pool.

Atherton is fast becoming the ultimate cycling destination with the growing popularity of the Atherton Forest Mountain Bike Park, a network of world-class, purpose-built, single-track mountain bike trails located in the Herberton Range State Forest and easy access from Atherton's CBD.

From its beginnings as a timber workers camp and staging post between the tin mines and the coast, Atherton has blossomed like its trademark jacaranda trees.

Today this diverse regional service centre has so many well-presented homes and streets it's regularly in the running for Australia's Tidy Town awards.

The region has a wealth of artists whose works are best seen at the Tablelands Regional Gallery.

Any visit should include checking out the wonderful pre-war Barron Valley Hotel, browsing through the town's quaint shops like Atherton Antiques & Australiana and enjoying a picnic at Hallorans Hill.

And right in the middle of town is one of the most remarkable and novel attractions anywhere in Australia.

Share one man's passion for crystals and fossils at the Crystal Caves in Main Street. Journey through 300m2 of tunnels and grottos that Rene Boissevain built to feature his million year old natural crystals and prehistoric fossils. Take a self-guided tour and marvel at the interactive displays which you can touch. Take photographs of the crystals, crawl around the exhibits and become a geological explorer. There's even on opportunity to crack a geode kind of a Kinder Surprise volcanic egg.

Just out of Atherton is an attraction which combines the two of the world's taste sensations dairy and chocolate. Savour the gourmet cheeses and chocolates, and let the children see how milk is made!

Also close by is Hasties Swamp, a seasonal wetland and national park which has an annual cycle of wet and dry, attracting a range of more than 300 resident and migrant birds. The two-storey Nyleta (the park's Indigenous name) Wetlands Bird Hide has wheelchair access on the lower section.

Celebrating Chocolate
Coffee Works

Celebrate chocolate on any day of the week at Coffee Works, which is taking chocolate to some very unusual places.

The imaginative chocolatiers at this Mareeba enterprise obviously have fun at work with varieties including orange polka dotted Jaffer Basher, lemon myrtle and lime and black pepper.

Walk through their doors and they promise decadent dark, wicked white and magnificent milk chocolate creations.

For the romantics this chocolaterie makes several types of chocolate hearts and for something different, how about a chocolate pizza birthday cake seeing is believing!

Coffee Works also offers visitors a look at coffee roasting and the opportunity to try several brews. The company now showcases the Australian coffee industry to more than 180,000 visitors annually in its stores including outlets in Mareeba and Atherton. It is considered a coffee connoisseurs 'heaven' synonymous with exclusive gourmet products, including its delicious chocolates.

Gallo Dairyland
The Gallo family business has been on the Atherton Tablelands for almost 100 years. Today the family farm spreads across 1000 acres of rich red volcanic soil and milking on average 350 cows a twice a day.

The freshest ingredients are guaranteed in these sweet treats which take the age-old craft of chocolateering and give it a Tropical North Queensland twist.

The chocolates taste of the lush tropics with flavours such as mango, pistachio, macadamia and passionfruit plus traditional favourites such as peppermint, hazelnut, cherry and orange.

The treats are given an extra taste boost being made with couverture chocolate that has a very high percentage of cocoa butter, typically between 32 and 39 per cent. It makes for a richer and smoother product. After being blended and tempered the results make for a chocolate with a glossy finish and a hard crisp consistency.

The chocolates at Gallo Dairyland look special and taste even better. Gallo's highly skilled chocolatiers make all the product by hand on the premises so you know you'll get a yummy mouthful on site but phenomenal chocolates to take away as a gift or savour later.

Located on the Malanda-Atherton Road, Gallo Dairyland is a licenced café known for its cheese tasting and sales as well as morning and afternoon teas and ice cream treats.

Sweet Farm Tours

Australian grown cocoa and vanilla and a working sugar cane farm make this farm gate experiencer a real sweetie.

Very educational and even more delicious, the Sweet Farm Tours are led by an actual farmer and let you touch and smell and try cocoa pods, cocoa beans, cocoa nibs and sugarcane.

After the tour there's Australian origin chocolate tastings. Daintree Estates, which runs Sweet Farm Tours, was the first commercial manufacturer of chocolate to use cocoa grown in Australia. It is also one of the few plantation-to-plate cocoa / chocolate producers so they have total control over every stage of processing.

The difference is evident in the final taste of the chocolate. See for yourself with a visit to this amazing and beautiful farm in the middle of a rainforest. You will leave extremely knowledgeable about cocoa bean production and with all chocolate cravings satisfied.

There's also locally grown vanilla to taste and as an added bonus, Sweet Farm Tours grows koala feed for a nearby sanctuary protecting these endangered animals.

Sweet Farm Tours is situated in the Whyanbeel Valley on the Miallo Bamboo Creek Road near Mossman at the northern edge of the Tablelands.

Atherton Tablelands Wonders That Will Take Your Breath Away

Trees

Singularly and en masse, trees on the Atherton Tablelands will leave you amazed and enthralled. Kuranda, the "village in the jungle" is just that, a town made lovely by its rainforest cloak. Lakes Barrine and Eacham, the volcanic twins, are both surrounded by rainforest, which gives them an otherworldly atmosphere.

The two famous strangler fig tees Cathedral and Curtain give every visitor that "oh wow" moment. Look up the best of the Atherton Tablelands is often over your head.

Trees are so special up here they even have their own kangaroo, and let's not forget the fruit and coffee trees that will take your breath away with amazing food and drink.

Waterfalls
Don't listen to TLC do go chasing waterfalls. The Atherton Tablelands has a whole circuit of them. Guaranteed to take your breath away and that's a relief on a warm summer day.

The Atherton Tablelands waterfalls are so beautiful they have even starred in tv advertisements.

Make a day of travelling round. The "official" waterfall circuit begins at Millaa Millaa on the Palmerston Highway and includes Zillie, Elliniaa and Mungalli Falls. Nearer Ravenshoe are the Soutia and Pepina Falls and Millstream Falls, Australia's widest.

Whether its sitting at the base of a waterfall mesmerised by the cascade falling down a sheer rock face, rock hopping over granite boulders or lazily paddling round a pool, the Atherton Tablelands' waterfalls are magic.

Chillagoe Caves
These limestone caves are a natural wonder of the outback. This limestone has been weathered, dissolved and re-formed by water to create spectacular caverns and passages, decorated by stalactites, stalagmites and flowstones.

Several of the caves are lit and look like rock cathedrals, while the Royal Arch is dark and a little spooky. Spiders with glow in the dark eyes and bats add to the atmosphere.

This is the quintessential Aussie outback pretty close to town. It takes about two hours from Mareeba and with the last 32km a mixture of dirt road and bitumen you know you are getting a dinky di bush experience. Check suitability during the summer period if you don't have a 4WD.

Tours are the way to go to ensure you see everything and spend a couple of hours with a very informative guide. There are three different tours available and its best to book. Or have a fossick round by yourself on a self-guide tour so take a torch.

Bushwalks, swimming in the local creek and having a meal in the pub with the locals are all part of an unforgettable experience.

Take a moment to look at balancing rock, the old smelter and some of the Indigenous art sites.

This is one breathtaking experience for the whole family, the kids will be awed along with the adults. And a bonus the caves are nice and cool inside.

Four hundred million years in the making, the Chillagoe Caves are one of the best kept secrets of Tropical North Queensland.

Innot Hot Springs
Hot springs in Tropical North Queensland? Bit coals to Newcastle? Hardly. To beat the heat and humidity what could be more divine than soothing a travel weary body in warm waters from a natural spring. The very definition of bliss.

Winding through the landscape between Ravenshoe and Mt Garnet is Nettle Creek, heated by natural geothermal mineral springs.

The waters in the creek are said to have therapeutic powers and were once bottled and shipped to Europe. They are an unexpected treat in this varied landscape but be careful, the water in some parts of the creek can reach 75 degrees. Ask the locals where the cooler places are along the stream.

Nearby Innot Hot Springs takes advantage of the natural heating and offer visitors a range of soaking options in six pools. The indoor and outdoor pools offer a dip ranging from searing hot to bath temperature to icy cold. The pools are close to a caravan park and dotted around a lovely setting.

And if you are feeling rejuvenated and fizzing to go, try some bird watching or gem fossicking in the region. It's famous for both.

Undara Experience
Like nothing else on earth, the Undara Lava Tubes at Mount Surprise are fascinating grottoes formed by volcanic activity.

Rock arches, extensive tunnels and underground lakes were all formed by an eruption about 190,000 years ago. The tubes were pushed out by molten lava, the top, outer-layer of the flow cooled and formed a crust, while the molten lava below drained outwards, leaving behind a series of hollow tubes.

Undara in the Ewamian language of the area means long way this is one of the most extensive lava tube cave systems in the world.

Up top are rich volcanic basalt soils covered by seasonal grasses and a ribbon of remnant dry rainforest.

Underneath are complex caves and tunnels there are more than 50 in the Undara National Park and surrounding area. In some the roof or walls have collapsed and flora and fauna have taken over. The tubes act like a giant drain for summer rain and Undara is considered one of the most biologically diverse cave systems in the world.

Access to the lava tubes is by guided walk only through the Undara Experience, a privately-owned business next to the national park. However, there are several self-guided walks in the region, including the 2.5km Kalkani Crater Rim trail, which takes you to the egg cup shaped rim and offers views across the lava plain to other volcanic vents.

The Undara Experience offers a range of accommodation options including huts, camping and caravanning sites, glamping and vintage railway carriages for a bit of fun.

Mountain Lakes. Barrine & Eacham

These twin tarns of the Atherton Tableland may look the same, dress the same but have very different personalities.

Formed by volcanic action thousands of years ago they are forest-fringed, cool-watered oasis' for the enthusiastic adventurer and Sunday-drive traveller alike in Crater Lakes National Park.

Both lakes are maars volcanic craters formed by a massive explosion from the superheating of groundwater. The lakes are clear and often bright blue/green in colour because they are only filled by rainwater; no streams or creeks run in to them.

Energetic Eacham

Lake Eacham is the more bumptious of the two. Lots of people swim here and the lake frontage near the car park has easy access to the water, a big swathe of grass for sun bathing or a kick round and tables for picnicking. A pontoon is provided for swimmers. There's a perimeter walk of 3km round the foreshore, which will take an hour or so but just take a short stroll down the path and you'll see fish and maybe turtles in the clear water. There's also a 1.4 km children's walk with playful activities on the way.

If you want to get out further on the 65-metre-deep lake pack a kayak or a paddle board. No motorised craft are allowed on either lake. Lake Eacham is reached by a short drive through a forest grove, perfect for a shaded run or ramble. More than 180 species of birds have been recorded in the area so you won't be lonely.

Serene Barrine

Lake Barrine is relaxation personified. Take a seat in its charming tea house and be mesmerised by the view out over the water to the old-growth rainforest all around. You have found your happy place. The lake is also about 65 metres deep and about a 1km wide. Indigenous people named it Barany. At 730m above sea level it has the look of an alpine lake albeit with tropical foliage.

The tea house is the second thing you notice about the lake, after its beauty. Built in 1926 it has a great possie at the edge of the water take morning or afternoon smoko of tea and scones on the veranda for the full tea house experience. The gardens are worth a look.

The lake has boat trips round the edge of this volcanic crater's brim to get to know the fascinating tropical ecosystem better. Birdlife galore, eels, turtles, fish and the occasional python.

Even on dry land it's easy to see scores of fishlife in the clear waters. And if you want to explore under you own steam there is an easy grade 5km circuit track or check out a couple of substantial kauri on a short stroll from the car park.

You can swim at Lake Barrine as well. Both lakes are signposted off Gillies Highway not far from Yungaburra.

Chillagoe to Mutchilba

Late in the 1800's when work was scarce and transportation was limited, miners often used to travel about the region using a wheelbarrow to carry all of their possessions. In 2004, as a tribute to these early pioneers and to honour their amazing trail-blazing feats, the road between

Mareeba and Chillagoe was named the Wheelbarrow Way.

Today a journey along the Wheelbarrow Way takes the traveller through rich farmlands and wooded Savannah country. All but 20km of the road close to Chillagoe are sealed and travellers should be on the lookout for cattle and horse which wander freely across the unfenced road.

Mutchilba: Mutchilba is a small farming community approximately 34km west of Mareeba, well known for its large production of mangoes.

Dimbulah: Further west on the Mareeba-Dimbulah Road is the township of Dimbulah. Dimbulah has a memorial hall, local shops, a hotel, caravan park, soccer ground, bowling club and swimming facilities.

Mount Mulligan: Fifty three kilometres north of Dimbulah on the Mount Mulligan Road is the former mining town of Mount Mulligan, the site of Queensland's worst mining disaster. Opened in 1910, the mine closed after an underground explosion killed 75 miners all the miners in the town. It reopened in 1923 and continued in production until 1957 when a hydro-electric scheme eliminated the need for the coal. Mount Mulligan is quite simply spectacular with its 18km ridge that is ten times larger than Uluru.

Petford: The locality takes its name from the railway station named after John Joseph Petford, an official of the Queensland Railway Department for many years.

Almaden: Almaden is a township with a population of 71 (2016 Census) and is on the railway line between Mareeba and the mining and cattle town of Mungana.

The town is an overnight stop for the Savannahlander train which operates between Cairns and Forsayth.

Chillagoe: Chillagoe is a genuine outback town with fascinating attractions and abundant wildlife.

When you arrive in town you will instantly notice the tall chimney at the ruins of the old smelter which is iconic to Chillagoe. Entry is free and there is a viewing platform and car park on a high vantage point with informative plaques.

The site is a great photo opportunity and there's fascinating information on how the pioneers toiled in those days.

Today there are many surviving historic points of interest around Chillagoe to be explored at your own leisure. Check out the Railway Station, bank vault, Court House, Police Museum, Post Office and Post Office Hotel.

There is so much to see and do that to fully experience, go back in time and immerse yourself in the history of Chillagoe a two nights stay is recommended.

AVIS and Budget car rental allow their conventional vehicles to drive to Chillagoe but not further westward beyond Chillagoe.

Kuranda

The picturesque mountain retreat of Kuranda Village is just 25km northwest of Cairns and attracts visitors from all over the world who enjoy its superb wildlife attractions, walking trails, river cruises, souvenir shopping and artists' galleries. Initially people came to admire the mighty 125m Barron Falls, while artisans were attracted to the region's natural beauty and decided to call it home, creating a vibrant arts and craft culture.

Make sure you allow plenty of time to visit some of Kuranda's world renowned attractions and activities, which include koalas, butterflies, native and exotic birds, kangaroos, reptiles, some of the world's most venomous snakes, and even come face to face with a huge life size replica of an Allosaurus Dinosaur.

You can see traditional Indigenous dance performances, voyage on a riverboat along the spectacular Barron River, get your photo taken holding a koala, feed wallabies and explore an amazing gemstone museum, all amongst the beautiful rainforest that envelops the town.

Kuranda has evolved into a superb place to shop. There are bargains to be had, as well as exquisite artisan pieces at the other end of the spectrum.

The markets in Kuranda are diverse and have been a feature of the village for 25 years, opening all year round except Christmas Day. Best Kuranda buys are the hand-made local products and quality Australiana such as opals, wood-art, didgeridoos and other authentic Indigenous artefacts. You'll find delightfully soft and supple kangaroo skins and leather products, and for that souvenir t-shirt for anyone back home, you can't go past Kuranda's range and prices!

Historic buildings now house a variety of upmarket eateries and bars to enjoy and relax in. Dine indoors in air-conditioned comfort, or take an alfresco table surrounded by the vistas and sounds of Kuranda at one of the many quality hotels, restaurants, cafes, bar and grills in this exciting village.

History
Kuranda began life in the 1800s as a retreat where locals could escape the heat and humidity of Cairns and the tropical coast. During the '60s, a new wave

of settlers arrived, embracing the alternative lifestyle movement of the day and establishing Kuranda as an arts and crafts nexus. Catering for visitors forms the basis of commerce and lifestyle in Kuranda today. There is plenty of accommodation to be found, whether it be a cosy bed and breakfast, a well maintained, multi-choice accommodation and camping park, an historic hotel that harks back to the 1920s or a modern resort with one of the best natural style swimming pools found anywhere.

Herberton & Irvinebank

Herberton
Herberton is 75 km west of Innisfail, 60 km south-west of Cairns and just 18 km from Atherton situated on the Wild River.

Herberton is the oldest town on the Atherton Tablelands and its entire precinct is listed on the National Heritage Register.

Historic Village Herberton is an astounding collection of Australiana in an historic hamlet of more than 50 buildings on the edge of the Herberton township. Spanning two centuries, the dwellings, vehicles, memorabilia and antiques which fill this cultural asset have been meticulously resurrected and inventively displayed. Among many treasures in this vintage village are a fully restored 1926 rail ambulance and a genuine pioneer's slab hut built in 1870. The original Herberton State School from 1881 is a perfect place to take the children and show them the pews and slates yesteryear's pupils made do with.

The Herberton Mining Museum and Information Centre occupies the site of the first big tin discovery in Australia, the Great Northern Mine. The centre has themed areas telling the fascinating story of Herberton's mining history and the town's development. There are mineral collections on display plus a small theatre for multi-media displays. Exhibits are being added regularly, and the young and not so young can try their hand at tin panning. The centre is also the starting point for The Great Northern Walking Trails, a series of self-guided walks of various lengths and challenges.

Irvinebank

The Herberton-Petford road leads to heritage-listed Irvinebank, the tin mining town that refused to die. Established in 1882, it boasts many century old buildings such as the home of the town's founder John Moffat, said to be the oldest Queenslander in the State. A courthouse and cellblock, the 1901 School of Arts Hall, Tramway

Station, the Queensland National Bank Building, Mango Cottage and the 1907 Post Office building all attest to the architecture of prosperity at the turn of last century. The Mighty Vulcan mine became the mainstay of the town, yielding the purest available tin in the world displayed at the 1907 London World Expo.

Visitors can also see the Mill and Treatment Works on the foreshore of Loudoun Weir and visit the renowned Loudoun House Museum in John Moffat's house. Pioneer graves can be matched with local history at the museum.

Malanda

Malanda, home to Malanda Falls and great for bird watching, bushwalking, and scenic drives.
Malanda is located 85 km from Cairns and 732 metres (2,402 ft) above sea level. The town is

located downstream of the Malanda Falls on the North Johnstone River.

Malanda is well known for its rainforest walks, panoramic views, wildlife and a very successful dairy industry. It is also home to the heritage-listed Majestic Picture Theatre, known as the oldest continually-operating cinema in Australia.

Malanda Falls Conservation Park: Malanda Falls, on the North Johnstone River, tumbles over basalt rock formed by an ancient lava flow that spread from the Mount Hypipamee area 15km away. There are two short walks through the surrounding remnant rainforest.

Rainforest Dreaming Guided Walk: Join local Ngadjon guide, Drew Morta, on a 45-minute Rainforest Dreaming Guided walk through the Malanda Falls rainforests and see the forest through the eyes of the local Ngadjon people.

Small group sizes ensure a personal and very special indigenous experience.

Self-guided walks: Two easy walks meander through the rainforests. Allow half an hour to an hour for each walk. Early in the morning and later in the afternoon are the best times to go birding, but tree-kangaroos are just as easily seen during the day.

Winfield Park: 3.9km from Malanda on Lake Barrine Road, is Winfield Park, a large grassed area next to the Johnstone River with picnic tables, BBQs and public toilets.

Bromfield Swamp: Not far from Malanda on Upper Barron Road is the extinct volcanic crater known as Bromfield Swamp. Each winter hundreds of cranes come to roost. This is a must-see for birders and anyone looking to be enchanted by the dancing displays of the Saras cranes. Early in the morning, or their fly-in at dusk are the best viewing opportunities.

Bartle Frere trail, Wooroonooran National Park: Climbing the summit of Queensland's highest mountain offers a challenging way to explore part of the World Heritage-listed rainforest of the Bellenden Ker Range.

Mount Bartle Frere is 1611m and is covered in rainforest from foothills to summit.

Mareeba

Gateway to Cape York and Food Lovers Paradise

A multi-cultural district rich in wildlife, museums, coffee and wine, with clear blue skies perfect for flying, Mareeba has a rich history going back to the gold mining days.

Couple that with a strong sense of community that hosts a Multi-Cultural Festival each August and embraces traditional outback sports such as the famous Mareeba Rodeo and The Great Wheelbarrow Race and you have a fun, vibrant and thriving stop off point.

The region is a magnet for selfdrive visitors, and a popular destination for Grey Nomads who enjoy Mareeba as a base to explore the Atherton Tablelands. It's also a gateway to Cape York and Gulf destinations.

Food Lovers Paradise
The region is the fertile food bowl of the tropics, as well as producing more than 70% of Australia's coffee crop and a fruit wine or two.

At the Coffee Works at Mareeba, follow the story of coffee from plant to cup and visit Coffee World, an antiquities museum housing a world class collection of coffee and tea memorabilia.

Visit Australia's oldest coffee plantation at Skybury, and enjoy a cup of their trademark coffee while taking in the unforgettable view from their cafe Skybury Farmgate.

And for something a little different, why not sip specially created house blends at Jaques Australian Coffee Plantation, an established estate where you can also take a plantation tour (or even a scenic flight in a microlight!).

Fruit wines are another specialty of the Mareeba region.

The Golden Pride Winery will introduce you to the delights of mango with their range which includes sparkling wine, port and liqueurs and is widely available throughout the region. At de Brueys Boutique Winery, taste the fabulous fermentations of lychee, mango, jaboticaba, bush cherry, mulberry, passionfruit and star apple.

Stop at one of the well-stocked roadside stalls and pick up a basket of produce, visit one of the food producers' cellar door style establishments, or make a reservation and enjoy the service at one of the region's restaurants, hotels or cafes. Savour and enjoy!

Hot Air Ballooning
Start your day by watching the sun rise over the rolling hills of the majestic Atherton Tablelands, then experience the wonder, silence and romance of floating in a hot air balloon. From the minute you arrive, you'll be part of the unique spectacle of many large colourful balloons standing ready for take-off at dawn.

Enjoy the 360-degree panorama of a hot air balloon ride over the varied landscape of the

Tablelands before coming gently back to earth. Afterwards, there's pack up games and the chance to check out the photos for sale of your ballooning experience both in-flight and personal portraits. Nothing compares to starting the day in Far North Queensland with a breathtaking ride in the oldest form of flight. This morning tour is highly recommended, excellent value and sure to be a highlight of your holiday here on the Atherton Tablelands.

Davies Creek Mountain Bike Park
This network of mountain bike trails in the Lamb Range between Mareeba and Kuranda is accessed from the Kennedy Highway, approximately 13km from Mareeba. Follow the Davies Creek signs. The trails wind along the rain-shadowed slopes of the Lamb Range.

With lengths and grades for everyone, riders navigate granite outcrops, cross clear streams, and traverse forests of bloodwoods, stringybarks, she-oaks, cycads and grass trees.

These shared trails were built for mountain bike riding but are available to walkers. Horse and trail bike riding are not permitted.

Millaa Millaa

Home to panoramic views and the famous waterfalls circuit.

Millaa Millaa is situated on the southern area of the Atherton Tablelands, about 60km west of Innisfail and 98 kms from Cairns. Driving from Innisfail take the Palmerston Highway or travelling from Malanda on the Malanda-Millaa Millaa Road, the township is 23.7 km away or 20 minutes drive.

This beautiful town is gateway to the southern Atherton Tablelands. Images of its multiple picturesque waterfalls have graced thousands of travel pages. At 850 metres above sea level, the town is nestled among emerald hills surrounded by lush dairy pastures, majestic rainforests and those magnificent cascades.

The 17-kilometre waterfall circuit and rainforest-clad Wooroonooran National Park are just two of the natural attractions that bring visitors to the mild climate of this town.

The circuit begins at Teresa Creek Road, just south of the township of Millaa Millaa encompassing Millaa Millaa Falls, Zillie Falls and Ellinjaa Falls. Together, these falls are the most photographed waterfalls in Australia.

Millaa Millaa Falls: Travelling south from Millaa Millaa on the Palmerston Highway, turn left onto Theresa Creek Road and about 1 km is the turnoff. There's good signposting to Millaa Millaa Falls.

Millaa Millaa Falls are a popular swimming spot...and good for spotting wildlife. Look for the Ulysses butterfly and platypus late in the afternoon.

Facilities include picnic tables, BBQs, shelters, public toilets and change rooms.

Zillie Falls: Zillie Falls are 7.5km from Millaa Millaa Falls. A viewing platform provides a photographic advantage and facilities include a BBQ and shelter shed in the carpark.

Elinjaa Falls: Ellinjaa Falls, 3 km on from Zillie Falls, flow over a series of lava columns.

The carpark has BBQ and picnic tables.

Walk down to the zig zag track to the stream great tree ferns and vines on the descent.

Pepina Falls: Ten kilometres from Millaa Millaa along the the old Palmerston Highway (now a scenic route) towards Ravenshoe are the Pepina Falls.

A short walk gets you to the base of these falls. Parking is very limited.

Mungalli Falls: Thirteen kilometres from Millaa Millaa along the Palmerston Highway, towards Innisfail is Junction Road and then follow the signs to Mungalli Falls. At 90 metres they are the highest on the Atherton Tablelands.

Misty Mountains: Millaa Millaa is the gateway to the wilderness walking tracks Misty Mountain Trails, Australia's first network of long distance walking trails in high altitude rainforest. More than 130 km of tracks have been constructed under a unique partnership between the region's shires, Queensland Parks and Wildlife Service (QPWS), the land's Traditional Owners, and volunteers from Conservation Volunteers Australia.

Millaa Millaa Lookout: One of the most superb vistas in the region unfolds from the Millaa Millaa Lookout on East Evelyn Road, Millaa Millaa.

Mount Molloy to Julatten

Mount Molloy: Just 30 minutes from Mareeba on the Mulligan Highway, is the historic mining and timber town of Mount Molloy. At its height Mount Molloy was a copper mine in the 1890s, named after Patrick Molloy who found the copper outcrop while searching for stray bullocks.

Today, this small town with a population of around 300, is much more humble with a bakery, general store and petrol station. Its main industry is cattle grazing, however tourism is growing steadily as visitors discover the beauty, wildlife and history of this area and its surrounding towns of Julatten, Maryfarms and Mt Carbine.

One historic site located at the south-east corner of the Mount Molloy cemetery near the mature grevillea tree is the resting place of prospector and explorer James (Venture) Mulligan. A very condensed but beautiful biography of his life can be read on his tombstone. Visitors can also visit the old steam engine that was used to supply the power to the local sawmill, which is located at the southern entrance to Mount Molloy.

The Mareeba region is acknowledged by birding experts as the richest region for birdlife in Australia. Nearly half of Australia's 750 bird species can be found here, and birders have recorded more than 300 species within a 15 km radius of nearby Mount Molloy.

Julatten: Tucked away in the rainforest just to the west of the popular coastal town of Port Douglas and just 10 minutes from its neighbour Mount Molloy is Julatten.

This small town attracts thousands of birders each year, on the lookout for species that include Spectacled Monarchs, Pale-Yellow Robins, Lesser Sooty Owl, Red-Necked Crakes, Pied Monarch, Yellow-Breasted Boatbill, and Orange-Footed Scrubfowl.

In summer, the spectacular Buff-Breasted Paradise Kingfisher is another highlight.

Mount Lewis: Nearby is the Mount Lewis Forest Reserve, home to some of the most accessible and scenic upland rainforest in the area. It is known as a good spot for birdwatching, where Golden Bowerbirds, Noisy Pittas, Blue-Faced Parrot Finches and Chowchillas can be seen.

Maryfarms: On the way to Mt Carbine when travelling north is the small town that was once known as Maryfarms. Birders, bushwalkers, astronomers, photographers, campers, anglers and four wheel drivers can choose to stay at Bustard Downs offering farmstay and bed and breakfast accommodation options as well as caravan and camp sites.

Mount Carbine: Further along you will reach Mt Carbine, another historic town dating back to the 1890s when Wolframite was discovered on Carbine Hill. Mt Carbine Caravan Park is ideally located for the traveller wishing to explore the Palmer River Gold Fields, Lakeland Downs with its vast cropping areas, the Annan Gorge, and the Mt Mulligan Coal Free Van Storagefield.

Ravenshoe to Mount Garnett

Ravenshoe

Ravenshoe, pronounced Ravens-hoe, is the highest town in Queensland at 920m above sea level. It has a population is about 1000 people in the township and many more in the surrounding area.

Situated on top of the Great Dividing Range, Ravenshoe sits between the Wet Tropics World Heritage rainforests to the east and the drier, open forests of the Gulf Savannah to the west. Ravenshoe is surrounded by natural wonders like Millstream Falls and Lake Koombooloomba.

Ravenshoe is the highest point of the Misty Mountains walking tracks network, and is a great location for wildlife watching, particularly for platypus, 12 species of possums, 340 bird species and of course, Lumholtz's tree kangaroo which is just one of 14 species of kangaroo to be found in the area.

Historically Ravenshoe was a town with a proud heritage of extracting timber from the surrounding forests. Since 1987, when the government world heritage listed 900,000 hectares (2,200,000 acres) of surrounding rainforest, the main industries have been tourism, beef and dairy farming.

The locals live a lifestyle to be envied, and celebrate it every year in the annual *Torimba Festival of the Forest* in October.

Windy Hill Wind Farm
Windy Hill Wind Farm was the first wind farm to be built in Queensland. It generates enough electricity to supply about 3500 homes equivalent to the population of nearby towns of Atherton and Mareeba. Created on the extinct Windy Hill volcano in 2000, its 20 wind turbines take advantage of the consistent winds on the volcano's slopes.

On a clear day, the views from the lookout platform are spectacular, taking in the farming countryside right through to the coast.

Koombooloomba Dam

From Ravenshoe travel south on Tully Falls Road to Koombooloomba National Park and Conversation Park. This sealed and unsealed road travels through Tully Falls National Park before reaching the boundary of Koombooloomba National Park, 20km from Ravenshoe.

There are three camping opportunities in Koombooloomba National Park and Conservation Park. Bush camp along Nitchaga Creek and Wall Creek roads in Koombooloomba National Park or in the defined bush camping area on the waterfront. Koombooloomba Conservation Park has a camping area with defined sites and some facilities. Camping permits are required.

Koombooloomba Dam is popular with water skiers and anglers. The dam is not part of the national park.

Millstream Falls

Big Millstream Falls is reputedly the widest single-drop waterfall in Australia. A walking track leads to a viewing area over the falls. A separate entrance to the park leads to Little Millstream Falls. View these beautiful falls from just near the carpark or take the steep and narrow track to their base.

Innot Hot Springs

Located between Ravenshoe and Mount Garnet on the Kennedy Highway is Innot Springs. The hot springs of Nettle Creek have long been established as rejuvenating and healing and the water was even bottled and shipped to Europe a hundred years ago.

Five kilometres north-west of Innot Hot Springs, Mount Gibson is popular with fossickers for its gem topaz. Camping is not permitted and a fossicking licence is required.

Mount Garnett

Mount Garnet is a small town on the Savannah Way and attracts gold fossickers and gem collectors. Originally founded on the discovery of copper and garnets in 1882, mining operations continued until the early 1900s when the Mount Garnet Freehold Copper and Silver Mining Company closed. The town languished until tin mining began in 1928 and several cattle stations and farms were settled.

Today zinc, copper, lead, silver and lime are mined in the area.

Wurruma Swamp
Wurruma Swamp attracts an amazing range of bird life and at certain times of the year there are thousands of blacks swans on the waters. The swamp retains water long after other local wetlands have dried up and is used for a water supply to the township.

Tinaroo

Lake Tinaroo is a very popular spot for swimmers, skiers, walkers, fishing (permit required), red clawing, ideal for picnics with barbecues available and has five camping areas located around the back of the dam in the Danbulla State Forest.

Tinaroo is a small settlement of accommodation and private residences on the edge of Lake Tinaroo and has developed into one of the region's most popular tourist locations that has so much to offer everyone.

Enthusiasts in sailing, skiing, swimming, fishing, red clawing, bird watching, walking, are all attracted to this town.

Or for a more leisurely pastime, take a relaxing stroll along the jetty to see the dam spillway or enjoy one of the many picnic spots in the area.

Tinaroo Dam was constructed in 1952 when the Barron River was dammed to supply irrigation water to farming areas of the Atherton Tablelands.

Lake Tinaroo is open all year for those chasing the famous sportsfish, barramundi. It is part of a fish stocking scheme, and permits are required to fish with the fee contributing to the scheme).

Permits and bait can be purchased from the caravan park in the township of Tinaroo.

Danbulla National Park
Get to Danbulla National Park via 28km of unsealed forest drive through plantations of pine and eucalypt trees, as well as rainforest with lovely views of the lake. Stay in one of the five camping areas along Danbulla Road and enjoy the unique features of the area including crater lakes, strangler fig trees, rainforest walks and places of

important local history and interest. Camping permits are required and fees apply.

Cathedral Fig
The Cathedral Fig Tree is a gigantic 500 year old strangler fig tree. Located in the Danbulla State Forest, the Cathedral Fig has the reputation of being the best place to hear the early morning bird chorus on the Atherton Tablelands.

Tolga & Walkamin

Tolga
The township of Tolga is a quaint village with good examples of early Queensland architecture and is about eight kilometres from Atherton along the rainforest canopied Kennedy Highway.

Tolga is in a partial rain shadow from the nearby Bellenden Ker Range. A centre strip in the main street features a towering fig tree as well as a heritage and timber display consisting of seven carved poles, much like totem poles. The creative carving showcases aspects of the Atherton Tableland's rich heritage including Indigenous culture, animals, plants and threats to the rainforest habitat.

With its range of accommodation from caravan parks, motels to a five star retreat, and displays of art work by local people it is an interesting little township.

Close by is Rocky Creek Memorial Park, which is dedicated to the thousands of soldiers who were stationed in this area during World War Two. With its many plaques on display, it is a popular stop over for many travellers.

Walkamin

Walkamin was built during the construction of Tinaroo Dam in the 1950s. Described as food bowl country, the site for the town was chosen due to its perfectly balanced weather patterns with the ideal climate for a wide variety of crops anything from mangoes, peanuts, bananas and avocados to coffee and tequila (well agave).

Yungaburra & Crater Lakes

Yungaburra is a picturesque village, largely unchanged since 1910. With 18 heritage-listed buildings, it is the biggest National Trust village in Queensland.

Yungaburra takes its name from the Yidinyji language, meaning a place of enquiring or questioning. The European settlement of Yungaburra spans from the early 1880s, but the history goes back much further.

Visit charming cafes, award winning restaurants and arts and crafts galleries to complete the picture.

Yungaburra's high profile landmark, the amazing Curtain Fig Tree, is only minutes from the village and is accessed by a short boardwalk from the sealed road.

Bushwalking is the ideal way to encounter the wildlife of the surrounding areas. A network of easy and moderate walking tracks will lead you through wetlands, rainforest, scrub and lakeside paths.

One of Yungaburra's main attractions is the Peterson Creek walking circuit where there are often platypus to be spotted. A re-vegetation program has ensured the tree kangaroo is also making its home there. The platypus viewing platform at Peterson Creek provides another spot for observing these elusive creatures.

Nearby Lake Tinaroo is popular for water skiing, fishing and family picnics. On the fourth Saturday of each month the famous Yungaburra Arts & Crafts Markets, the largest and most popular of all the region's country markets, are held on the green in the village centre.

Avenue of Honour: The Afghanistan Avenue of Honour is a living memorial dedicated to the memory of all who served in the fight against terror in Afghanistan and to those brave and selfless Australians who made the ultimate sacrifice in defence of freedom and liberty.

The Afghanistan Avenue of Honour made up of Illawara Flame Trees is located at Tinaburra, 3km from Yungaburra Village.

Crater Lakes National Park: The volcanic features of the landscape on this part of the Atherton Tableland are between 10,000 (Pleistocene) and two million (Pliocene) years old.

Ten minutes from Yungaburra is Crater Lakes National Park and home to Lake Eacham and Lake Barrine.

Camping, including sleeping in campervans and vehicles, is not permitted within Crater Lakes National Park.

Lake Eacham: Lake Eacham is a maar a volcanic crater formed by two massive explosions from superheating of groundwater. This vent now forms the catchment of the lake and is 65m deep. Some of the original underlying sedimentary rocks occur today as metamorphic rock outcrops in parts of the crater rim. No streams flow into or out of the lake, with water only lost through seepage and evaporation.

The water level can fluctuate 4m between wet and dry seasons. Indigenous stories of the explosion of Lake Eacham describe the forest at the time as "open scrub". A subsequent study of pollen records from lake sediments supplements this view, suggesting the rainforest formed on the Atherton Tablelands only around 7600 years ago.

In 1988 Lake Eacham was included within the Wet Tropics World Heritage Area (WTWHA) and in 1994 joined Lake Barrine under a single protected area Crater Lakes National Park.

Lake Eacham is a clear, blue lake surrounded by lush rainforest and offers swimming, birdwatching, canoeing, picnic areas and shady walking tracks. It is a popular recreation area for locals and visitors.

The Aboriginal Traditional Owners of Lake Eacham welcome you to their country and ask that you respect their special place.

Lake Barrine: Lake Barrine was formed over 17,000 years ago when a large volcano erupted, leaving a crater that over time filled up with water to create a lake. The crater was formed as a result of a series of volcanic explosions. These explosions were caused by the hot molten rock coming into contact with groundwater. This caused a build-up of steam, gases and pressure which blasted the central core from the volcano. This massive explosion left a huge crater, which filled with rainwater to create Lake Barrine.

A walking track around the lake allows for forest-fringed, secluded views of the lake and excellent opportunities for viewing wildlife. A pair of towering bull kauri pine trees, over 45m tall, is a feature of the park.

Lake cruises operate from the privately-owned Lake Barrine Teahouse offering visitors a relaxed view of the lake and its wildlife.

Activities, Sights and Tour

Four-wheel Drive Adventures Beyond Mareeba

These 3 tracks are the epitome of the Atherton Tablelands four wheel driving big country and big fun

Rugged Beauty

The Mount Haig Circuit aka the Tinaroo Range Roads takes to some magnificent bush country and several sweet swimming spots. Find Emerald Creek Falls Rd via Tinaroo Creek Rd and Cobra Rd. Stop at the falls if its swim time; soon afterwards you will start to ascend the Tinaroo Ranges. After 12km take Mount Edith Rd, which undulates through rose gum and casuarina forest before descending to the headwaters of Emerald Creek. Time for a swim or a wander through the rainforest. Jump back in your truck for a climb between Mount Edith and Mount Haig. The road winds along until it intersects with Dunbulla (Tinaroo Road). Take the right-hand option and follow for two clicks before turning right into Kauri Creek Road, which will take you back to the start of this 40km circuit.

River Crossings Galore
Change gears for the Clohesy River Road. The track is easy and fun for the family. There're 10 creek crossings making it an adventure for the novice 4WDriver. You may not need all the gears but you will need decent clearance. Best not tackle it in the wet. The track goes through Dinden State Forest and is signposted off the Kennedy Highway about 20km on the right driving from Mareeba. There are lots of places to stop and enjoy the atmosphere, including the Clohesy boardwalk, which takes you to a mighty fig tree. Look out for cassowaries, feral pigs and other wildlife. The road is not a circuit but it does connect to the Copperlode Dam/Lake Morris access road, which needs a permit to use. The trip is about 20km return.

Mine Some History

If you are looking for a full day out try some of the historical mining routes on the Atherton Tablelands such as this circuit drive. From Mareeba head to Petford it's about an hour. Turn left at Lappa, a few kilometres out of Petford. Then take the left-hand fork. This is the Lappa/Mount Garnet Rd, which will turn into Nymbool Rd. You'll see plenty of evidence of tin mining in this region and as well just after the old town of Gilmore you might be able to make out Abdul Wade's Camel Track. Abdul Wade, an Afghani camel trader, and his 500 camels made a flat line track across the landscape to Mount Garnet.

You will next hit California Creek, a 4WD low range water crossing which may be impassable in the wet. There's a view of the Tate Valley coming up on the right and you'll be grinding to the top of the Great Dividing Range at 763m. Shortly afterwards the road joins Kennedy Highway and you can reward yourself at Innot Hot Springs before heading back to Mareeba on the bitumen or else take Coolgarra Rd to head back to Petford. After 13 km you will pass the old Fingertown Mine and drive through Coolgarra Station (please shut gate) and be heading to Irvinebank. From Irvinebank take the Herberton-Petford Rd. Look out for the working Porphry mine and the bleached white quartz cliffs of Elizabeth Bluffs.

Free diving Lake Eacham

Lake Eacham has long been a popular spot for sporting enthusiasts from all different walks, but there is a new trend taking to its crystal clear shores and this one involves holding your breath. Tanya Snelling finds out more:

Five minutes with ... Lisa Mattes from Apnea Cairns

1. What does apnea mean?

Apnea is ancient Greek (apnoea) and means "not breathing". In this context, it describes freediving, diving on one breath.

2. Why do you freedive in Lake Eacham?

The lake has perfect conditions for freediving. You can access its 65m depth within a few minutes of swimming, there are no currents or big waves disturbing your relaxation and you also won't have any boats coming too close to you, except for the odd kayak here and there.

3. 65m, wow how deep can you go?

I have freedived to 47m in the past, and if you do the first level course, you will freedive to a maximum of 20m.

4. How long can you hold your breath?

My personal best in static apnea (floating on the surface, face down) is 5.22. You can easily train to improve your own breath holding times, just make sure to stick to rule number 1 always dive with a buddy, even if you are in your bath tub.

5. Why do you keep doing this, don't you feel the need to breathe?

Freediving is like meditation for me and one that always works. Once you are in the water, you forget about what bothered you before, things to do later, you are just here in the now and that is a truly blissful feeling.

Atherton Tablelands has full spread of events

The picturesque Atherton Tablelands has a calendar crammed with events, adventure and entertainment in coming months.

Whether you like a rodeo, rock concert, the races or a regatta, there is something for everyone, set against some of the most beautiful and diverse landscapes in Australia.

Tropical Tablelands Tourism chair Ghis Gallo said the full season of events officially kicks off in Kuranda with Easter in the Park, a free event for children of all ages.

On Easter Saturday (March 31) it will rain eggs in the rainforest, with 15,000 chocolate treats dropped from the skies. The eggs are dropped on the hour from 11am to 2pm in Centenary Park with a Golden Egg in each batch.

"The lucky finders win an amazing Kuranda prize package, and the under 5s won't be lost in the egg scramble, with a special place for the littlies to meet the Easter Bunny and collect their own bag of eggs," Ms Gallo said.

Kuranda's Easter in the Park starts at 10am and includes a magic show, Pamagirri Aboriginal dance performance, candy making demonstrations, a Dream State Circus show, egg and spoon and sack races, face painting, three bouncy castles and horse and carriage rides plus stalls and much more.

Fancy a rock concert amongst the stunning contours and colours of the Outback? Over April 20-22, Undara Outback Rock & Blues is an amazing weekend of music and mates in the extraordinary lava tube country.

And they're racing at Mount Garnet from May 4-6. It's also the annual rodeo and a chance to let your hair down and party. After the thoroughbred racing and one day rodeo, the nightly socialising round a campfire make the event a real Atherton Tablelands treat.

Recent rain has filled Lake Tinaroo, a good omen for the 50th Tinaroo May Day Regatta on May 5.

Each year in early May sailors from all over North Queensland converge on Lake Tinaroo in the central Atherton Tablelands for what is regarded as one of the most enjoyable regattas in Queensland.

Step back in time at the Historic Village Herberton for Pioneer Weekend on Saturday and Sunday, May 5-6. Families of all ages are invited to join in at the replica mining town and have a go at tin panning, try their skills at sack races and the egg and spoon challenge, or strut their stuff in period costume for Fashions on the Field.

Since it started in 2004 the 140km Great Wheelbarrow Race has raised more than $1.5 million for charity and this year's push from

Chillagoe to Mareeba will be as popular and punishing as ever.

Described by one participant as "hands down the best thing I've ever done" the team relay race follows the Wheelbarrow Way, originally the route miners would take pushing all their belongings in a wheelbarrow. Running from May 18-20 on the Atherton Tablelands, the race is a unique experience for participants, supporters and spectators alike.

The Chillagoe Rodeo (May 11-12) also known as the Bushman's Carnival, has an Ultimate Cowboy Challenge on the Friday night and a Saturday bursting with barrel racing, steer wrestling, bronc busting and bull rides.

Other events on the calendar include the Dimbulah Lions Festival (May 26), The Malanda Show (July 6-8), The Atherton Show (July 9 &10), the Mareeba

Rodeo & Festival (June 30-July 15) and Christmas in July at the end of July.

Lake Barrine

The Tea's as Good as the View

The teahouse at Lake Barrine may be 80 years old but the Devonshire teas it serves are as fresh and inviting as the crisp Atherton Tablelands air around this charming landmark.

The teahouse juts out over the clean, clear waters of Lake Barrine, which sits right in the middle of tropical rainforest and is protected within the Crater Lakes National Park.

It's a welcome stop on any Atherton Tablelands tour and one of the most beautiful places to have a cuppa or light lunch anywhere in Australia.

And for lovers of a good Devonshire Tea, Lake Barrine offers one of the most memorable; where else could you get locally grown tea AND coffee, scones made to a fourth-generation secret recipe and topped with cream and jam produced in the neighbourhood as well.

Visitors can sit back on the balcony and enjoy the scenery or be entertained with a lake cruise of the volcanic crater brim.

Lake Barrine was formed when water filled the crater left by a volcanic eruption about 15,000 years ago.

The lake is 730 m above sea level, about one kilometre in diameter, has a shoreline of almost 4.5 km, which can be walked and an average depth of 65m.

The 45-minute guided boat tour circumnavigates the lake, getting its passengers up close and personal with the history, geology and wildlife of the lake.

But Lake Barrine is more than just a pretty spot it has been looked after for nearly 100 years by one family the Currys.

With a lease granted in perpetuity in the 1920s for the teahouse site, four generations have kept the area pristine in this captivating part of the Atherton Tablelands.

The teahouse itself has had a series of incarnations dance hall, aquatic centre, guest house, school, convalescent home but is now a unique facility for those who want to walk, swim, cruise or just drink in the amazing serenity and beauty of Lake Barrine.

Lake Barrine is off the Gillies Range Road, about 10kms from Yungaburra.

Geological-Wonders
Mt Hypipamee

The Hypipamee crater is referred to as a volcanic pipe. The pipe was opened upward through surface rocks by gas produced from molten rock below and as a result of tremendous pressure, the vent exploded sending volcanic bombs far across the landscape. It has a diameter of 61 metres at the water level which is 58 metres below the platform. Even 85 metres below the water surface, the pipe hasn't lost any of its dimensions.

Crater Track

Meander along a 800 metre return (30 minutes) rainforest track and emerge at the viewing platform overlooking the sheer granite walls of the crater.

Hallorans Hill, Atherton

Hallorans Hills Conservation Park protects eucalypt forest and a remnant of the endangered mabi forest on an extinct volcanic cone. The cone is part of the legacy of the tableland's fiery geological past.

Enjoy the 1.4km walk to the top of the hill or drive there through suburban Atherton. The expansive views from the summit exhibit the tableland's mosaic of land use and geological formations.

A council park at the summit adjoins the conservation park and provides barbecues, toilets, tables, play equipment, walking track and interpretive signs.

*Best times are early morning or late afternoon when you can watch the sun set.
*Walking track takes approximately two hours return.
*Hallorans Hill Conservation Park has no wheelchair-accessible facilities.
*Some wheelchair-accessible facilities are available in the adjacent council park on the summit.

The Crystal Caves

Discover one of the world's most extraordinary Crystal and Fossil Collections.

Share one man's passion for crystals and fossils at the Crystal Caves. Journey through 300m2 of tunnels and grottos that Rene built to feature his million year old natural crystals and prehistoric fossils. Take a self-guided tour and marvel at the interactive displays which allow you to touch and photograph the crystals, you can even crack your own!

Journey through Rene's manmade tunnels and grottos as you share his passion of natural crystals and prehistoric fossils on a self-guided tour of the Crystal Caves. Covering an area of 300 sq meters, the interactive displays allow you to touch and photograph over 600 specimens.

Hiking and Walking

Short Walks

Want to really get out onto the Atherton Tablelands? Head out on foot for a diverse range of self- powered short walks. Here's a couple of short excursions to start with:

Two quick walks that entice a long slow WOW out of visitors are strolls to the Curtain and Cathedral fig trees. They are both massive and they are both near Yungaburra.

- ➢ The Curtain Fig is on the handily named Curtain Fig Road off Gillies Highway on the way to Atherton. It's a 10 minute easy walk to the strangler fig tree and there's a boardwalk round it.

- ➢ The Cathedral Fig is off Danbulla Forest Drive an extension of Boar Pocket Road. It's about 15 minutes walk and easy going. Chance of spotting wildlife at both places are pretty good.

A shortish walk near Ravenshoe will reward you with views of the widest single drop falls in Australia. Big Millstream Falls are at the end of a 340 metre track and it takes about 10 minutes to get to the lookout. The falls are in eucalyptus woodland and there are side trails to discover the area's rich World War II history. You can also walk to Little Millstream Falls down a steep track and be rewarded with a swim. Take Tully Falls Road and then Wooroora Road.

Hallorans Hill in Atherton takes you through mixed eucalyptus and Mabi forest so plenty of shade. It's tops for bird watching and has excellent views from the summit. This moderate walk of 3km will take about an hour and a half. Not for novices. The walk starts in Hallorans Hill Conservation Park, off Louise Street, Atherton.

5 Awesome Spring Hiking Adventures

Want to really get out among the awesome Atherton Tablelands, and like a decent trek? Try one of these longer walks to get you amongst some incredible backblocks country.

Atherton Tablelands Rail Trail

If you are ready to stretch your legs try the 20.5km Atherton Tablelands Rail Trail. It takes you through rich agricultural landscape and some patches of endangered Mabi rainforest. The trail has both well interpreted indigenous history and extensive WWII info. It's a gentle track, with a slight fall to the north. Start at either Platypus Park near Atherton or Walkamin.

Summit Mount Emerald

If you are set for something more strenuous the 9.5km to summit Mount Emerald and back should get your heart pumping. There are great views of the vast Atherton Tablelands at the top but on the way hikers pass through eucalyptus forest along the Great Dividing Range. There's also a plane wreck, remnants of a tragic 1990 crash. It is difficult and allow about 5 hours. From Atherton, find Anderson Road and go 2km to its end, the hike starts on the right-hand side of the road.

Ramble round Lake Barrine

Like your hiking flat-ish? The circuit of Lake Barrine is long enough at 5kms for a decent walk and will take about 120 minutes and is moderate going. But it's shaded the whole way, set alongside a volcanic crater lake. Look out for giant Kauri pines and the abundant wildlife, particularly birds. Reward yourself with smoko at the Tea House when you return. Lake Barrine is just off the Gillies Highway, 9km east of Yungaburra.

Conquer Mount Bartle Frere

If you are a serious hiker and that means very, very skilled think about a two-day hike to the top of Mount Bartle Frere. You need to be fit, experienced and well prepared. You also need to book a camping permit. The weather is very changeable and can be very harsh. The trail is unformed and you will have to scramble in some places. But the rewards and they are rewards on climbing Queensland's highest mountain on a good day are uninterrupted views from the Atherton Tablelands to the coast, plus passing through amazing rainforest that few people disturb on the way up this 1611m peak. Access through Topaz, near Malanda.

Mt Hypipamee treasure

If you are in the Herberton region Mt Hypipamee National Park has several rainforest walks that will take you into amazing volcanic country without too much effort. The Crater Track and Dinner Falls Circuit lead to a viewing platform above the volcanic pipe created by gas explosions. The tube (or hole in the ground) with water at the bottom, is 61 metres across and 82 metres deep. The Crater Track is rated easy and 800m return while the picturesque Dinner Falls Circuit is longer at 1.2km and a little bit harder. Both start at the park's carpark just off the Kennedy Highway.

Top Spots: Lookouts to Look For

Want to get high? Visit these lookouts for the best views of the Tablelands.

Millaa Millaa Lookout

The peaceful and simply stunning Milla Milla Lookout will take your eyes from the Atherton

Tablelands to the coast on a really clear day. At 1070m its one of the best places to take in the beauty of the Tablelands with a 180 degree sweep from northwest to southeast. On McHugh Road, just a short hop from the Kennedy Highway.

Undara National Park

Undara National Park is known for what's underground but up top is pretty special too. Atkinson's Lookout is a south east facing granite slab giving exceptional views south to the Granites and Racecourse Hill the highest shelf volcanic cone in Undara. The lookout carpark is next to the airport and it's an easy walk to the rock and the stunning outlook.

Balancing Rock, Chillagoe National Park

Balancing Rock Lookout has two for the price of one; a panorama of bush country and the puzzling Balancing Rock Itself just how is it staying perched there? This spot is about 2.5km drive from Chillagoe and it's a short walk form the carpark to the rock and lookout. The vantage point gives wide views of the whole Chillagoe region.

Balancing Rock Lookout has two for the price of one; a panorama of bush country and the puzzling Balancing Rock itself just how is it staying perched there? This spot is about 2.5km drive from Chillagoe and it's a short walk form the carpark to the rock and lookout. The vantage point gives wide views of the whole Chillagoe region.

Mt Lewis Lookout (near Mt Carbine)

The Mt Lewis Lookout up the Rex Range is the icing on the cake of a four-wheel drive adventure. Take the Mossman-Mt Molloy Road and climb 28km to 1200m. Be on the lookout for wildlife as well as the gobsmacking view; this part of the world is renowned for spectacular fauna and flora, some of it right on the road.

Mt Wallum

Possibly the highest point you can easily drive to in all of Queensland. The Mt Wallum lookout near Atherton is at 1292 metres and gives amazing views in almost all directions of the Atherton Tablelands. Look for signs to the south of Atherton along the Herberton Road for this vantage point.

Barron Falls Lookout

Best in the wet, but impressive all year round. The view out over Barron Falls near Kuranda shouldn't be missed. You get a good look at the falls and dam at top as well as the gondola gliding over the Kuranda Range and the train tracks cut through the bush. The lookout is signposted from the town and very accessible for everyone.

World War 2 Trail

For World War II buffs or descendants of servicemen a tour of the Atherton Tablelands transforms into an engaging history trail. More than 100,000 troops were based in 160 sites around the Atherton Tablelands from 1942.

With a cooler climate than Cairns, the area still provided excellent jungle warfare training for those heading off to places like (Papua) New Guinea and Bougainville. Servicemen were also treated for malaria at camp hospitals. The Atherton Tablelands was the largest Australian military base with camps at Tinaroo, Kairi, Wongabel, Herberton, Wondecia, Ravenshoe, and Mt Garnet as well as Atherton / Tolga area.

Make a poignant start at the Atherton War Cemetery, the third largest in Queensland. On the corner of Rockley Rd and Kennedy Highway, it contains 164 graves of soldiers and airmen. The graves follow the principles set down by the War Graves Commission permanent, uniform headstones with no distinction for military or civil rank. It also has a Cross of Sacrifice, the elegant signifier of Commonwealth War cemeteries.

Rocky Creek at nearby Tolga is home to a major memorial and old hospital complex. Rocky Creek War Memorial Park is the site of the 2/2 Australian General Hospital, laundry and medical stores site. The hospital treated more than 30,000 patients from 1943-45. There are 94 unit plaques around the park. There is an overnight stopping area for self-contained motor homes and caravans for $5 a night.

A nearby "igloo" was used for films, concerts and dances. It's rumoured Hollywood star Bob Hope once performed there Road to Rocky Creek maybe? It was later a cane factory and family home before falling into disrepair and is now a refurbishment project by Tablelands Regional Council. You'll find both on the Kennedy Highway just outside of Tolga.

If you head north to Mareeba you'll find the site of a busy WWII airfield. Mareeba Airfield was renamed Hoevet Airfield by the Americans after one of their own Major "Pinky" Hoevet was killed in 1942. It was home to American bombardment and fighter squadrons and later the RAAF. There is a memorial at the airfield, which is about 4kms south of the town.

Going south, between Atherton and Ravenshoe there are many historical markers along the roads, identifying the campsites of various units.

Just west of Ravenshoe is Millstream Falls National Park where you can combine WWII fossicking with waterfall watching and maybe a swim. The park is rich in WWII history as more than 1000 men from 7th and 9th Divisions lived here mostly in tent accommodation. Sites, walking tracks, concrete slabs, trenches, corduroy roads and training and parade grounds are clearly evident. As is occasionally a bit of live ordinance don't touch!

If you want to mix your history with a little light refreshment, Atherton RSL has a Japanese 37mm anti-tank gun on display outside and Mareeba RSL has a 70mm mountain gun. Both were captured in Bougainville.

And Rainforestation near Kuranda has an inimitable way of getting you round the bush on a fleet of restored WWII army ducks. Be transported back to the jungles of Papua New Guinea and Bougainville on these tough old amphibious six-wheel drive vehicles as you tour the rainforest and lake.

Birding and Wildlife

Birding Birdwatching on the Atherton Tablelands attracts global attention due to the diverse avifauna and variety of local habitats, including riverine, wetland, woodland, rainforest, grassland, agricultural and parkland.

Top birdwatching spots include the dryer regions of Mt Molloy and Kaban, Nyleta Bird Hide (Hasties Swamp National Park), Nardello's Lagoon, Bromfield Swamp, Abattoir Swamp, the National Parks of Mt Hypipamee, Crater Lakes, Davies Creek, Barron Falls, Mt Lewis, Mareeba Wetlands and the Wongabel State Forest.

October to April may be the region's hotter and wetter months, but it is also the time when the migrant species arrive from Papua New Guinea, including the beautiful Buff-breasted Paradise Kingfisher, Channel-billed Cuckoo and Common Koel.

Many birds such as the White-eared Monarch and Noisy Pitta are also breeding at this time of year and are easier to observe as they search for food. During the cooler, drier, winter months from May to September, Victoria's Riflebirds are also displaying

At this time, Brolgas and Sarus Cranes can also be found on the Atherton Tablelands feeding on the harvested agricultural fields

Unique Wildlife encounters The Bat Hospital in Atherton is internationally known and has a visitor centre where you can see and learn more about microbats and flying foxes. You can also take in the wildlife at excellent attractions such as Skyrail Rainforest Cableway and Hartley's Crocodile

Adventures. If you look very hard, you may spot a Lumholtz's or Bennett's Tree Kangaroo up high in the branches or platypus in freshwater lagoons.

Eyes on Wildlife will help you uncover the hidden wonders of the region's most stunning rainforests. With personalised itineraries, your host Patrick will make sure you see the birds and other wildlife you travelled here for, while also allowing time for photography.

Snapping Tours offers unique and picturesque boat cruises along Innisfail's Johnstone River. Their love of wildlife and interest in the history and knowledge of the local area has set the foundation for creating exciting and interesting cruises.

There are more than 430 bird species in the Wet Tropics and the Great Barrier Reef and 327 of these can be seen on the Atherton Tablelands.

Touring

Want to explore all that the Atherton Tablelands and beyond has to offer but prefer to sit back, relax and let someone else do the work? Choosing a guided tour can be a lot of fun and ensures you get the most out of your visit, learning a lot about local culture, art and history along the way. Tours also offer the chance to meet other like-minded travellers and of course the friendly locals.

Food tastings Brett's Outback Tasting Adventures offers unique and exclusive food experiences that allow you to savour regional foods at their source and hear the stories behind the foods. Departing from Cairns and Port Douglas, you will travel across the Atherton Tablelands where you will sample locally grown coffee, wine, cheese and more.

The rugged outback Let Billy Tea Safaris take you to the Chillagoe Caves and outback with stops at Mt Uncle Distillery and Mareeba Wetlands.

Touring Visit Sweet Farm Tours, in the Whyanbeel Valley just north of Mossman.

It offers a great experience on a working sugarcane farm and cocoa plantation. Learn how cocoa is grown in Tropical North Queensland and discover for yourself why its Daintree Estates Chocolate is becoming known as one of Australia's best. Rainforest Heart, near Millaa Millaa, will also introduce you to new flavours with one of its Australian tropical bush food orchard tours.

Travel further north to the prehistoric Daintree Rainforest with a stop at the Daintree Discovery Centre a must. This award-winning world class interpretive facility allows visitors easy access to every level of the rainforest, from the forest floor to the upper-most reaches of the canopy. The animated, life-size dinosaurs, bugs and fish will also keep the kids entertained for hours.

Attractions No journey would be complete without a visit to Hartley's Crocodile Adventures. See the big crocs up close during feeding times as well as experience the wetland boat rides and wildlife presentations.

Hartley's is family friendly and offers a three-day return pass.

Transport For travel further afield, Trans North provides an excellent service. It offers three return trips weekly from Cairns to Karumba connecting at Undara, as well as six return services weekly from Cairns to Cooktown, including an inland service via Mareeba and Lakeland.

The all rounder Tropic Wings Cairns Tours & Charters offers a range of tour options.

Destinations include Kuranda, with Kuranda Scenic Railway, Skyrail, Rainforestation Nature Park and Australian Butterfly Sanctuary. Cape Tribulation and the Daintree are also included in their tours.

National Parks Guide

There are more than 30 national parks associated with the Wet Tropics World Heritage Area. Bellenden Ker, now part of Wooroonooran National Park, was created in 1913, followed by Hinchinbrook Island in 1932 and Lake Barrine and Lake Eacham (now Crater Lakes National Park) in 1934. Parks on the Atherton Tablelands cover a diverse range of landscapes. They serve to protect our native plants and wildlife and are places to learn about our environment, heritage and culture.

Barron Gorge National Park and Speewah Conservation Park.

With rugged landscapes, lush rainforest and spectacular views, this is a park not to be missed. Near Kuranda, the impressive Barron River tumbles 250m down a series of ledges and spills into the gorge below.

Davies Creek and Dinden National Parks, Bare Hill Conservation Park and Dinden West Forest Reserve. Between Kuranda and Mareeba, discover some of the region's best kept- secrets in national parks straddling the Lamb Range, the mountainous backdrop to Cairns. Granite outcrops, towering forests and boulder-strewn creeks are highlights.

Crater Lakes National Park

Refresh in the clear blue, rainforest- fringed waters of Lake Barrine and Lake Eacham extinct volcanic craters up to 65m deep. Laze around the water's edge with your picnic, watching the kids swim and play. Take a stroll around the lake and marvel at the 1000-year old, 50m tall twin Kauri Pine trees at Lake Barrine.

Danbulla Forest Drive

Set aside at least a day to explore the spectacular Danbulla National Park and State Forest.

With forests, plantations and World Heritage-listed rainforest, this 12,000ha park is nestled between the Tinaroo and Lamb ranges and stretches along the banks of Lake Tinaroo.

Hallorans Hill Conservation Park and Wongabel State Forest: Hallorans Hill and Wongabel State Forest are home to Lumholtz's Tree Kangaroos. At Hallorans Hill in Atherton township, walk through eucalypt forest and endangered rainforest to the summit of this volcanic cone for stunning views over the Atherton Tablelands.

Mount Hypipamee National Park:

Explore the Crater track and emerge from high-altitude rainforest to the surprising sight of a diatreme (volcanic pipe). Try to imagine the sounds and sights of the massive explosion that formed this crater. Use a spotlight to see possums, tree kangaroos, spiders, leaf- tailed geckos and insects at night.

Millstream National Park
Explore the World War II heritage walk and see the remains of tent sites, corduroy roads, training and parade grounds, trenches and other reminders of the military role the region played in the war years.

Ancien Rainforest

Journey back in time, long before the dinosaurs roamed, to discover the history and natural beauty of North Queensland's World Heritage-listed rainforest.

Representing one of the world's most ecologically fascinating and diverse environments, the ancient rainforest of North Queensland is recognised as the oldest continually surviving tropical rainforest on Earth, with a range of plant and animal lineages dating back hundreds of millions of years in some cases.

From mosses and lichens to basket ferns, native orchids, strangler figs trees and the majestic Kauri Pine, the Wet Tropics bioregion is teeming with plant life more than 4000 species in fact. Add to this the range of rare and endemic animals such as Lumholtz's Tree Kangaroo, Torrent Tree Frog, Ulysses Butterfly and Southern Cassowary, and the uniqueness of the rainforest environment becomes even more apparent.

Hugging a narrow coastal fringe between Townsville and Cooktown adjacent to the Great

Barrier Reef - Australia's World Heritage rainforest accounts for a mere 0.12% of the entire Australian continent. While small in size, the area is very rich in natural and cultural values. Its prehistoric ancestry that is some 75 million years older than the Amazon provides a fascinating story of the Earth's history and evolutionary processes.

This rainforest is the birthplace of song birds, kangaroos and some of the world's first flowering plants.

It offers a window back in time where you can experience the sights, sounds, smells and natural beauty of what is arguably the most botanically diverse environments the world over.

One of the region's more thrilling means of experiencing and appreciating this landscape is the Skyrail Rainforest Cableway in Cairns.

The stunning 360 degree views are perfectly complemented by the unique perspective that Skyrail offers as it glides just metres above the pristine rainforest canopy before descending to explore the forest floor at the Red Peak and Barron Falls Stations.

Complimentary ranger-guided boardwalk tours, interpretive signage and scenic lookouts at Red Peak Station unlock the secrets of the ancient tropical landscape.

Discover more at Barron Falls Station via the interactive touch screens, displays, audio-visual and educational tools of the CSIRO Rainforest Interpretation Centre. Marvel at the rugged beauty of the Barron Gorge and majestic Barron Falls, and learn more about the area's pioneering past at the engaging historical display.

Discover, encounter and immerse yourself in what is arguably the world's most beautiful rainforest experience.

Getting Here

Tropical North Queensland has rightfully earned its reputation as one of the most beautiful and diverse localities to visit in the world and finding your way around has never been easier, with some fantastic tried and tested drive routes that all lead to the Atherton Tablelands and beyond.

Cooktown and Cape York
The push to the tip of Australia is a must for the intrepid road warrior. Visit amazing Aboriginal rock art and pioneer relics, marvel at nature in the national parks or try your luck sport fishing. The Palmer River Gold Fields, Lakeland Downs, the Annan Gorge, the mysterious Black Mountain and historic Cooktown all warrant further exploration.

Chillagoe and The Wheelbarrow Way

The Wheelbarrow Way encompasses some of the richest and most important history of our national heritage between Mareeba and Chillagoe.

Drive through ancient landscapes with spectacular escarpment formations and be sure not to miss the beautiful limestone caves at Chillagoe. Also spend some time in Chillagoe touring the historic copper mines of the Old State Smelters.

The Great Barrier Reef Drive

This drive takes in 140km of spectacular scenery, hugging the rugged coastline from Ellis Beach to Port Douglas, passing through Mossman and over the Daintree River before meandering through the World Heritage-listed Daintree Rainforest on the way to Cape Tribulation. Enjoy the brief ferry ride across the crocodile- filled Daintree River and prepare for the wild and untamed beauty that awaits.

Lake Tinaroo

At the very heart of the Atherton Tablelands is Lake Tinaroo.

With over 200km of shoreline, it offers fishing, sailing and water sports enthusiasts plenty of room to spread out. Each year more than 500,000 people visit the lake, which was built on the Barron River in the 1950s. Lush green scenery and deep, clear water affords the perfect backdrop for sailing, boating, canoeing, water skiing and more.

Recreational fishing is also popular with ample opportunity to catch a barramundi, sooty grunter, sleepy cod, mouth almighty, archer fish, spangled perch and many species of crayfish, including the red-claw and yabby. Fishing permits are required here.

Drive along the shores, stopping at Platypus Rock Lookout for a view over the lake and Atherton Tablelands.

Where to Stay Lake Tinaroo Holiday Park is a popular pet- friendly holiday spot with a range of accommodation options, including 47 waterfront villas, poolside, family and studio units, budget cabins and caravan and camp sites. Tinaroo Lake Resort is a stylish home-away-from home with all apartment balconies providing views of the lake. The resort has an outdoor pool, barbecue area, library, restaurant and bar so there are plenty of places to relax and unwind after a day out on the lake.

Crater Lakes

Swim in an ancient crater lake right here on the Atherton Tablelands. The twin volcanic crater lakes of Barrine and Eacham are tranquil pools of water fringed by rainforest. Formed approximately 12,000 years ago by violent volcanic eruptions, it took several hundred years for water to fill these giant craters and for the trees to grow back, creating the placid lakes used today by local families and visitors for recreation.

There are no streams that flow into or out of the lakes, water is lost only through soakage and evaporation and is only replenished by rain. Many people are surprised to discover the level can fluctuate by up to four metres between wet and dry seasons.

Lake Barrine. At Lake Barrine, the Heritage Teahouse Café offers a charming setting to enjoy tasty light lunches and Devonshire Teas the best home-made jam and sconces on the Atherton Tablelands.

Take time to enjoy the 45-minute guided Rainforest and Wildlife Cruise, which operates daily from 9.30am. This relaxing and informative cruise provides one of the few water-based tours in the area.

There is a short walk to the towering twin Kauri trees, thought to be over 1000 years old, while a longer 5km circuit, will take you along the shoreline.

Lake Eacham The clear blue and green waters of Lake Eacham make it a go-to-place on a summer's day and with motored craft banned, it's a serene and pristine beauty spot on the Atherton Tablelands all year round.

Surrounded by dense rainforest, it has an average depth of 65m. Access to the water is simple and there is a pontoon provided for those who want to play in the deeper water.

For those who don't want a dip, viewing platforms give a better look at this breathtaking lake and its inhabitants, including fish and turtles.

The tiny fish have been known to give visitors the spa treatment, nibbling at feet. Lake Eacham is a 10-minute drive (7km) from Yungaburra via State Route 52 (Gillies Range Highway) and Lakes Road. The drive through the rainforest is the perfect prequel to arriving at Lake Eacham where the enchanted forest gives way to a picture-book view.

There is a 3km walking track circling the lake and the area is renowned for birdwatching, not surprising given more than 180 species have been recorded within the upland rainforest.

There are picnic areas and barbecue facilities at lakeside and numerous places to take in the stunning scenery around the 50ha lake circumference.

Yunga Burra

Yungaburra, the historic heart of the Atherton Tablelands, is a quaint village established in 1890. With 18 heritage-listed buildings, it is the largest National Trust village in Queensland and with its lovely streetscapes largely unchanged from those early pioneer days it is easy to see why. Wide verandahs and historic shop fronts line the pretty lanes, while charming cafes, award-winning restaurants and arts and crafts galleries complete the picture.

Attractions Yungaburra's high profile landmark, the amazing Curtain Fig Tree, is only minutes from the village and is accessed by a short boardwalk from the sealed road. The Cathedral Fig Tree, another 500-year old strangler fig, is located in the nearby Danbulla State Forest.

The Lake Eacham Hotel, or Yungaburra Pub as it is commonly known, is a magnificent showpiece of federation architecture. Nick's Swiss-Italian Restaurant, an interesting Alpine-style chalet, has also become an attraction in this Australian country town.

Nearby Tinaburra Waters is popular for sports. It features a boat ramp and special areas set aside for water skiing and jet skiing. Active travellers will love exploring the lakes and trails by bike, boat or kayak. If you are looking for more adventure, hire a kayak, bike, or join a cycling tour.

Yungaburra Hospitality Yungaburra is something of a foodie heaven. Nick's Swiss Italian Restaurant comes highly recommended, with great food, wine and a wonderful, jovial atmosphere. The restaurant has been under the ownership of Nick Crameri for 32 years. NIck also offers free guided tours of his organic garden, explaining the workings of the worm garden and the different herbs grown and used.

Accommodation Charming B&B's such as Allumbah Pocket Cottages, Lakefront Holiday Villas, Birds 'n' Bloom Cottages and Blue Summit Hideaway can be found. Yungaburra Motel also offers comfortable self-contained units.

Activities Bushwalking is the ideal way to encounter the wildlife of the surrounding areas. A network of easy and moderate walking tracks leads through wetlands, rainforest, scrub and lakeside paths. The village is set below Mt Quincan, an extinct volcanic crater.

Visit the Peterson Creek Walking Circuit where there are nearly always platypus to be spotted. The re-vegetation program has ensured Lumholtz's Tree Kangaroos are also making their home there.

The platypus viewing platform also provides an excellent place to watch.

Shopping The village features a garden centre, boutiques, art and gem galleries, crafts and country style antiques, a popular second hand book store and a foodmart / newsagent / delicatessen. Today, the town's interests are fostered by the Yungaburra Business Association. For gorgeous handcrafted furniture, homewares and gifts visit Artistree Gallery.

History Yungaburra has existed largely unchanged since 1910 and the Eacham Historical Society has chronicled much of the town's early history. The town's original name was Allumbah Pocket and in the early days of the 1880s miners en-route to the tin and goldfields used the hamlet as an overnight stopover. Take a self-guided stroll around the village with an Old Town Loop map from the Visitor Information Centre.

Malanda

The pretty town of Malanda is situated in the heart of the Atherton Tablelands' rainforest region. It is great for bird watching, bushwalking and taking a cooling dip at the falls. As well as being the centre of a highly successful dairy industry, the village has many resident artists. Their work can be viewed on an art trail showcasing a series of vibrant mosaics depicting the town's history.

Malanda Attractions Take a break at the historic Malanda Hotel and step inside for a cool ale. The Malanda Dairy Centre in the main street features an innovative retro milk bar restaurant. Gallo Dairyland is also a must stop visit with delicious cheese and chocolate to sample and buy.

Malanda Accommodation Visitors have a range of accommodation options, including The Canopy Rainforest Treehouses and Wildlife Sanctuary.

Malanda Activities. The Malanda Falls Visitor Centre is a great place to start. Allow time to browse the fascinating displays, including its violent volcanic past, and learn about this unique tropical region, its natural history and its people. The area's traditional owners are the Ngadgon-ji people. Informative and highly personalised guided rainforests walks are available on weekends or by appointment at a small cost.

In the rainforest surrounding Malanda there have been more recorded daytime sightings of the rare Lumholtz's Tree Kangaroo than elsewhere. It is common to see platypus, turtles and lizards as well.

Two self-guided walking trails, the Tulip Oak Walk and the Rainforest Walk weave through the forest or along the banks of the North Johnstone River. Each walk takes approximately 30 minutes to enjoy and begins near the visitor information centre.

The beautiful Malanda Falls is a must-see stopover with year round swimming and picnicking. Not far from Malanda is Bromfield Swamp, an extinct volcanic crater. Hundreds of Sarus Cranes and Brolgas roost here each winter. It is a stopping point for bird enthusiasts hoping to see the enchanting dancing displays of these birds.

Millaa Millaa

Beautiful Millaa Millaa, known as the Village in the Mist, is the gateway to the southern Tablelands. The image of its picturesque waterfall has graced thousands of travel pages. At 850m above sea level, the town is nestled among emerald hills surrounded by lush dairy pastures, majestic rainforests and magnificent waterfalls.

Millaa Millaa Town The village is over 100 years old and its rich, rural heritage is outlined in the local museum. Don't miss the massive Kauri Pine logs, a memento of the logging industry of the past.

Next to the museum is a covered picnic area featuring a sculpture of the famed explorer, Christie Palmerston. One of the most superb vistas in the region can be seen from the Millaa Millaa Lookout just west of town.

Millaa Millaa Waterfalls Millaa Millaa's picturesque waterfalls, which have been attracting visitors for over a century, are Queensland Heritage- listed. The Waterfalls Circuit begins at Theresa Creek Road just east of town and the drive encompasses Millaa Millaa Falls, Zillie Falls and

Ellinjaa Falls. All the falls have walking tracks, however, Millaa Millaa Falls also has picnic tables, change rooms and toilets.

Other falls to visit include Pepina and Souita, which are located 10km from Millaa Millaa along the Old Palmerston Highway towards Ravenshoe.

From town, travel east 11km to Junction Road and follow the signs onto the Mungalli loop, which includes Mungalli Falls, the highest waterfall on the Atherton Tablelands.

Misty Mountain Trails Millaa Millaa is also the gateway to the Wet Tropics wilderness long distance walking trails. More than 130km of tracks have been constructed. This network of short and long wilderness tracks takes visitors through pristine, high-altitude rainforest with crystal clear creeks, waterfalls and panoramic views. These tracks are intended for visitors with medium to advanced bushwalking and navigation skills.

Gourmet Produce Don't miss the successful bio-dynamic/organic dairy, Mungalli Creek, where you can sample its range of award-winning products as well as watch them being made. A private guided tour of Rainforest Heart will offer you the chance to see first hand an operating tropical fruit farm, where Davidson's plum, lemon aspen, rainforest cherry and rainforest lychee are all grown.

Atherton

From its beginnings as a timber-getters' camp and staging post between the outback tin mines and the coast, Atherton has blossomed like its trademark Jacaranda trees into a diverse regional centre. Well known to the locals as a highland getaway destination, Atherton is also famous for its rich soils, which grow superb produce and flowers.

Attractions The region has a wealth of artists whose works are best seen at the Tablelands Regional Gallery. Check out the wonderful pre-war Barron Valley Hotel, browse through the town's quaint shops like Atherton Antiques & Australiana and enjoy a picnic at Halloran's Hill with a view of the Seven Sisters volcanic cones.

Hasties Swamp (Nyleta Wetlands) is a seasonal wetland with an annual wet and dry cycle. The two-storey bird hide provides wheelchair access on the lower section.

Take time to get to know the inhabitants at The Bat Hospital on the road to Herberton. Here, you can meet flying foxes and microbats at the visitor centre. This internationally renowned facility is operated by a not-for-profit group dedicated to the conservation of bats and their habitat. They rescue, rehabilitate and release hundreds of bats each year and the facility is open seasonally to the public.

The Crystal Caves In the main street, you will find one of the most remarkable and novel attractions in the whole of Australia.

The spectacular private mineral collection features more than 600 specimens, including rare crystals, gemstones and fossils.

These treasures have been brought together by one visionary who found love at first site more than 40 years ago after cracking his first geode along the banks of Agate Creek in North Queensland. Rene Boissevain and his wife Nelleke have made it their life's work to build one of the largest mineral collections in Australia. Don't miss the Empress of Uruguay, the world's largest amethyst geode.

Chinatown Gold attracted Chinese settlers to North Queensland in the late 1800s and when the gold ran out, many turned to timber cutting and market gardening. The remains of Atherton's Chinatown are now an archaeological site featuring the community's fully restored place of worship, the Hou Wang Temple. The Temple was the social and religious heart of Atherton's Chinese community. There was also a community hall, kitchen and pig oven. People gathered here to worship, celebrate festivals and discuss community issues.

The Temple is part of a complex featuring a Chinese museum with interactive displays of Atherton's Chinese heritage and a prized collection of original artefacts and historic photographs of the once bustling precinct.

The Chinatown grounds host regular markets and food festivals.

Agriculture The rich basalt soils of the Atherton Tablelands yield an amazing range of produce. Around the Atherton area small to large farming enterprises produce lettuce, strawberries, macadamia nuts, bananas, beans, maize, corn, sugar cane and avocados. Sample these at roadside stalls and take away a memory of the taste of farm fresh produce.

Accommodation Atherton has always featured as a service centre and a stopover point for travellers. Today, the Trans North transport service provides linkages between Atherton, Kuranda and Cairns all the way to Karumba via Undara. Visitors can enjoy comfortable accommodation at the Atherton Holiday Park or Halloran's Leisure Park.

Dining out The Atherton International Club is open seven days for lunch and dinner and is a great place to enjoy a buffet meal, steak, fish and chips and other Aussie favourites.

Herberton and Irvinebank

In the late 1880s, miners like John Moffat created a boom on the back of the tin they extracted from the bush clad hills.

Today, Herberton's well-preserved buildings and inviting streets are drawing people back with a new vibrancy. Connect with Australia's history and folklore by re-visiting the past.

HISTORIC VILLAGE HERBERTON The Historic Village Herberton provides a rare glimpse spanning two centuries into Australia's pioneering past and cultural history. Exhibits range from dwellings, antiques and vehicles through to Aboriginal artifacts and World War II memorabilia. It is a living museum experience, with demonstrations of vintage machinery and trades, including blacksmithing and printing.

The Village occupies 16 acres (6.5 hectares) at Herberton and has been laid out to resemble a tin mining town with a garage, newspaper office, butcher's shop, chemist, grocery store, frock salon, toy shop, coach house, John Deere tractor shed, radio store, sewing machine shop and tool shed. Each each stocked with period wares and items.

Elderslie House, built for John Newell, 'the father of Herberton', sits grandly among more than 60 restored buildings. These include the Herberton State School, circa 1883, and the 'haunted'

Bakerville Tearooms, where food is served daily. Allow a full day for your visit.

The Village is open seven days and dogs on leads are welcome.

Herberton Town The oldest town on the Atherton Tablelands has its entire precinct listed on the National Heritage Register, and is best discovered via its intriguing photo posts and self- guided Heritage Walk. See the earliest building, the 1881 School of Arts, in the main street and wander down to the Jack & Newell Store c.1882, which houses the fascinating Spy & Camera Museum.

Open seven days, this museum is one-of-a-kind and will transport visitors from downtown Herberton to the cold, dark streets of the former USSR and the world of espionage. Learn the history of photography, starting with the birth of today's modern camera and finish with owner Michael Peterson's favourite the spy camera.

THE RAILWAY MUSEUM Also worth a visit is the Railway Museum, located at the end of John Street. Open on weekends and public holidays, the museum is operated by The Atherton-Herberton Historic Railway Inc. volunteer organisation. Having restored the old train line, they now operate train rides from Herberton Station to the Historic Village Herberton on a regular Sunday timetable between 10am and 3pm.

The Herberton Mining Museum and Information Centre Occupying the site of the first big tin discovery at the Great Northern Mine, the museum has themed areas telling the fascinating story of Herberton's mining history and the town's development. There are mineral collections on show, plus a small theatre for multi-media displays.

Irvinebank Established in 1882, Irvinebank boasts many century- old buildings such as century-old buildings. These include Loudoun House, now a museum, and which was the home of the town's founder, John Moffat. At nearby Montalbion, a former Cobb & Co. stop, you can fish in the dam and camp under the stars.

Kuranda

Colourful and quirky, Kuranda is the place to find art, tropical handicrafts and jewellery made by local artisans. The Village in the Rainforest is one of the gateways to the Atherton Tablelands, where you can be entertained by buskers, dine at an array of restaurants, enjoy walking trails or a river cruise and experience the region's iconic nature-based attractions. Spend a few days here immersed in Kuranda's culture this vibrant community has both unique style and engaging sophistication.

Attractions One of Kuranda's most treasured landmarks is the Barron River and its spectacular gorge, home of the mighty Barron Falls. The Kuranda Riverboat Wildlife Spotting Cruise operates from beside the train and Skyrail arrival stations. During a 45-minute calm water cruise, spot freshwater crocodiles, turtles, snakes, water dragons, fish and many gorgeous tropical birds.

The Australian Butterfly Sanctuary, the largest butterfly flight aviary and exhibit in Australia, is a beautiful garden containing more than 1500 colourful butterflies. Birdworld Kuranda has one of the best single collections of free-flying birds in Australia with more than 300 species from around the world. BatReach is a rescue and rehabilitation centre operated by volunteers. It is located off the main street and admission is by donation.

Kuranda's Koala Gardens is ideal for visitors with limited time who want to see Australia's best known wildlife like koalas, wallabies, wombats, crocodiles and reptiles.

Shopping Over the years Kuranda has become a great place to shop. There are bargains to be had, as well as exquisite artisan pieces. Spend time browsing the unique stores or the delightful Kuranda Heritage Markets. There are diverse stalls at these markets, which have been a feature of the Village for 25 years.

Start your day here and take advantage of the free shuttle from the Skyrail / Kuranda Scenic Railway Station. These markets are all-weather and are open daily from 9.30am to 3.30pm. Inside, you will find souvenirs, art and craft, fashion and local wildlife attractions.

Many of the products sold in Kuranda are made by the people who live and work in the town. Whether it is an original painting, individually designed jewellery, locally made sweets or a handcrafted bowl, these unique gifts are sure to be perfect even for the person who has everything. Best Kuranda buys are the hand-made local products such as the Australian Bush Store.

Restaurants and Cafes Historic buildings from the past now house a variety of upmarket restaurants, cafes and bars. In between shopping, try the locally grown coffee, honey, macadamia nuts and homemade ice creams or sit back and relax at one of the cafes or restaurants dishing up everything from locally made pies to fresh reef fish.

Events Kuranda hosts two free community events each year The Kuranda Easter Festival and Kuranda Festival. The latter commemorates each October the official survey of Kuranda in 1888. The Kuranda Easter Festival has free activities for the whole family. These include magic shows, circus performances, German sausage eating competition and horse and carriage rides, celebrating everything that makes Kuranda such a unique and vibrant destination.

Kuranda Day sees the Village in the Rainforest come alive with unique competitions and free activities for the whole family. Key events include the annual Bash of the Barron River Raft Race, the Great Kuranda Undie Fun Run and the German Sausage Eating Competition.

History Kuranda has always been a magnet for visitors. The village began life in the 1800s as a retreat where locals could escape the heat and humidity of the tropical coast.

During the 1960s, a new wave of settlers arrived, embracing the alternative lifestyle movement of the day and establishing Kuranda as an arts and crafts nexus.

Catering for visitors, in one form or another, forms the basis of commerce and lifestyle in Kuranda today. There is plenty of accommodation to be found in and around Kuranda so plan to stay a while at one of the gorgeous B&Bs.

Around Kuranda The journey itself to Kuranda is an exciting one. Other than the scenic highway route, you can choose to make your way to Kuranda via two of the region's star attractions - the Kuranda Scenic Railway or Skyrail Rainforest Cableway. The railway line is an amazing engineering feat, crossing steep ravines on towering bridges and passing through numerous tunnels. The train stops at the spectacular Barron Falls on the way.

Skyrail's gondolas glide above the rainforest canopy, with stops at an interpretive centre and boardwalks into the lush forests. This is a not to be missed opportunity to learn about one of the most botanically fascinating and diverse areas.

Accommodation Choose from units, cottages, an artist's studio, cabins, dormitories, luxury rooms with modern conveniences, or just sleep in a tent. Enjoy breakfast in bed, cook your own, or eat out. The choices for overnight comfort are varied, from the Billabong Sanctuary to the quaint Ronday- Voo B&B, with tropical forest settings and access to water in pools and creeks adding to the experience.

Walking Trails Kuranda has a network of interlinked walks that provide access through the village and its surrounding environment, including Barron Gorge National Park.

The Village Walk showcases the main street and finishes at the site of the original Kuranda markets. Jumrum Creek Conservation Park is a walk through the rainforest while the Jungle Walk passes through a regenerating forest. The River Walk offers a pleasant riverside stroll down a tree-shaded esplanade. The walks are linked so that you can mix and match options to suit your interests and available time. At the start of each track is an introductory sign.

Tolga and Walkamin

Tropical North Queensland has rightfully earned its reputation as one of the most beautiful and diverse localities to visit in the world. Finding your way around has never been easier, with some fantastic tried and tested drive routes that all lead to the Atherton Tablelands and beyond.

Tolga. A thriving community today, Tolga began life as a simple staging post on the track linking the Herberton tinfields with Port Douglas.

During World War II, the region became a training centre and base for Allied forces.

Discover the past at the Tablelands Heritage Centre and at the Tolga Museum, which houses memorabilia of World War II and the local timber and agricultural industries, and at the Tablelands Heritage Centre.

Rocky Creek War Memorial Park. From 1943 to 1945 the Atherton Tablelands was the largest military base in Australia, hosting between 100,000 and 300,000 troops from 140 different units.

The Rocky Creek Memorial Park was established over a decade ago at what was the site of the largest field hospital in the southern hemisphere to honour servicemen and women.

Dedication ceremonies are held in the park each August on the Sunday nearest Victory in the Pacific (VP) Day. For further exploration into the region's war history, follow up your visit with

a trip to the Mareeba RSL, which has excellent historical displays.

Attractions Tolga is central, pretty and the ideal holiday base with a choice of budget accommodation. Tolga's foremost attraction is the established fine woodwork gallery, Tolga Woodworks, on the main road.

As well as exquisitely crafted, handmade timber pieces ranging from small spinning tops and bowls to fine furniture, the gallery features a large array of hand-forged iron and hammered steel pieces, ceramics, fused glass and silver jewellery.

These showcase the talents of Tropical North Queensland's finest artisans. There is also a great cafe, which serves lunches as well as morning and afternoon tea.

The Tolga racecourse is the venue for the markets, with a wide range of local produce and crafts on display on the first Sunday of every month.

As you drive south towards Atherton, the road passes through the Tolga Scrub, a delightful, short rainforested strip with a leafy canopy.

Walkamin Walkamin was built during the construction of Tinaroo Dam in the 1950s. Described as food bowl country, the site for the town was chosen due to its perfectly balanced weather patterns with the ideal climate for a wide variety of crops. Just north of Tolga, Nardello's

Lagoon is a peaceful retreat with waterbirds. Visit the Cellar Door and Bridges Bar & Restaurant nearby at Mt Uncle and sample the excellent liqueurs and spirits

Chillagoe and Petford

DID YOU KNOW?

About 400 million years ago Chillagoe was the site of a shallow sea with thriving coral reefs. Over time, the limestone formed by those ancient reefs has been folded, stretched, heated and weathered to form the jagged, glittering limestone bluffs and underground caves that characterise today's remarkable landscape.

Chillagoe is a genuine outback town with fascinating attractions and abundant wildlife. It is easily accessed by conventional vehicles via the Wheelbarrow Way

The Wheelbarrow Way, which starts at Mareeba, was named after the gold mining pioneers who, when work was scarce and transportation limited, trudged out bearing their worldly goods in a wheelbarrow. This is commemorated each May when runners compete in a fundraising footrace pushing a wheelbarrowthe 140km between Chillagoe and Mareeba. Dimbulah, the gateway to the gold fields, sprang up on the Walsh River to service the ore trains.

Once mining faded, cropping became the focus and today sugar cane, mango and lychee plantations can be seen. Almaden, Petford and Emuford are all linked by the Etheridge railway line, which welcomes the Savannahlander train on its weekly run from Cairns via Almaden and Mt Surprise to Forsayth.

Climb the range to the remains of the 100-year old Lappa Pub, another famed stopover of old. On entering the Chillagoe region, a dramatic landscape created by massive limestone bluffs and rock formations greets travellers.

Tours Billy Tea Safaris offer a fully inclusive one-day Chillagoe and outback day tour, so why not let someone else do the driving while you take in the history and amazing landscapes? Billy Tea departs Cairns and the Northern Beaches every Monday, Wednesday and Friday.

Swimming The Chillagoe Weir is a great swimming hole with plenty of shade and picnic tables. It is only a few minutes drive from the town centre (the turn off is on the road to the airport).

Savannah Way

The Etheridge region to the west of the Atherton Tablelands still echoes with the romance of the famous gold rush days that drew thousands of miners to try their luck at a series of sites from the mid-1860s. Relics of those days can still be found throughout the district and around the settlements of Mount Surprise, Einasleigh, Forsayth and Georgetown. Several goldfields, base metal fields and gem fields still excite fossickers today. The "poor man's" Etheridge goldfield, so-called because you don't need expensive equipment, has never been worked out. Modern day prospectors with metal detectors and hand tools find specimens such as coloured topaz, agates, sapphires, smoky quartz and other precious stones and gold nuggets.

Visitors to the region will enjoy getting off the beaten track, camping in remote locales by waterholes with giant paperbarks, bird watching, visiting historic ghost towns and simply enjoying the tranquillity amid the region's wooded savannah grasslands.

Mt Surprise is the first town encountered within the Gulf Savannah when travelling from the East. This railway town on the old Cairns to Forsayth line is an ideal area to fossick for gemstones, explore the Forty Mile Scrub National Park, cool off at Junction Creek just a few miles west, or swim in the Einasleigh River, especially in the early part of the year after the storms. Here you can see a wide range of gems on display and learn how faceting is done, join a dig at a local claim with expert guides or explore by yourself with hire equipment, mud map, fossicking licence and advice. The O'Brien's Creek designated fossicking area, 37km north of Mt Surprise, is a well-known topaz area and yields gorgeous stones.

The Undara lava fields west of Mt Surprise is the toe of the lava flow that originated from the 164 craters of the McBride Plateau. These are basalt tunnels, which run for some 160km underground and can be accessed only through the Savannah Guide Post located at the Undara Lava Lodge on the edge of the Undara Volcanic National Park.

You can take local day tours or take advantage of the camping and accommodation on offer. Guided tours can be organised either by Undara Experience or Bedrock Village.

Walk the path of an ancient volcano during the day then sleep cocooned in an antique railway carriage. Check the Undara Experience website for details of the famous Undara Opera in the Outback and the Undara Outback Rock and Blues events.

Forsayth is the rail terminus of the Savannahlander's four-day journey from Cairns. It is located within the Etheridge goldfield and adjacent to the Agate Creek Mineral Reserve.

Ask the locals about some of the mining relics you can see when you visit. The newly renovated Goldfields Hotel offers meals, accommodation, general store and fuel (diesel and unleaded).

Einasleigh is a tiny township originally named Copperfield, which began life after the discovery of copper in 1866. It is on the Savannahlander rail line and sits among some unusual scenery with flat top hills rising out of grasslands.

The Einasleigh Hotel is walking distance from the beautiful Copperfield Gorge. The town comes alive at the famous races and rodeo, usually held around Easter.

Georgetown sits west of the Newcastle Range and is the administrative centre for the region and a service centre for local pastoralists and mining operations.

Gold was discovered near here in the mid-1860s and a reminder of this is the Cumberland Chimney, 20km west of town. It is all that remains of the gold crushing plant it processed nearly 66,000 ounces built by Cornish masons. The adjoining dam is a great place for bird watching, especially in the dry season. The town is home to a motel, hotel and caravan parks

A must-see in Georgetown is the TerrEstrial Ted Elliott Mineral Collection of more than 4500 display specimens.

About 90km from Georgetown is the striking Cobbold Gorge, formed through sedimentation of the Hampstead Sandstone 134 million years ago and hewn by nature to leave permanent waterholes beneath spectacular cliffs. Cobbold

Gorge forms part of a working cattle property and access to the gorge is by Savannah Guide-led boat trip and tours. Camping, powered sites and cabins, meals and tours are all available through Cobbold Gorge Camping Village.

Another outpost in the Etheridge Shire is The Lynd Junction, about 80km from Einasleigh. Accommodation and meals are available at the roadhouse and caravan park, which boasts the Guinness Book of Records' smallest bar in the world.

Fossickers may be interested in the Moonstone Hill Resource Reserve, about 90km south of the Lynd Junction on the Kennedy Development Road.

The Etheridge region is an exciting, and romance at its core. Remember that any fossicking requires a permit and make sure you know where to dig as mining claims and mining leases are 'no-go' areas.

When you have had your fill of the excitement and discoveries of the rugged, red Savannah country, head of the Atherton Tablelands.

Cassowary Coast

The Cassowary Coast region provides a stunning gateway to the Atherton Tablelands with beautiful beaches, offshore islands, rainforest-fringed freshwater streams, majestic mountain ranges and rich seas and agricultural land producing food from fish and shellfish to vegetables, sugar cane, beef and ultra-tropical fruit.

Where better than the Cassowary Coast to see the endangered Southern Cassowary a two metre tall flightless bird and a key disperser of rainforest seeds? In a quirk of nature, it is the male cassowary that incubates the eggs and raises the chicks.

MISSION BEACH is one of the few places where the Wet Tropics and Great Barrier Reef World Heritage Areas meet. The reef is closer to Mission Beach than places further north and local firms offer reef fishing, snorkeling and diving trips, and sightseeing trips around the Family Islands, including famous Dunk Island. At Mission Beach you can "jump the beach", taking in a birds-eye view of the reef with a skydive before landing on the sand. Perhaps a rainforest or beachside walk is more your style, or simply relaxing and enjoying a delicious meal at an excellent local eatery.

Cassowary Coast is Australia's banana- growing hub and centre of a growing ultra-tropical fruit industry, with mangosteens (the 'queen of tropical fruit'), lychees, rambutans, guanabana (sour sop) and now cocoa, with a chocolate factory at Mission Beach.

It encompasses the larger towns of Innisfail, Tully, Cardwell and Mission Beach.

Tully is home to the famous 7.9 metre giant 'golden gumboot', sugar mill tours during the cane crushing season and white-water rafting.

Cardwell is the stepping off point for Hinchinbrook Island, the largest island national park in the southern hemisphere. It is also home to the Girringun Aboriginal Art Centre, representing artists from nine traditional owner groups.

Innisfail, the regional centre, is a pretty town built on the confluence of the North and South Johnstone rivers. In the wake of the 1918 cyclone, the town was rebuilt in the Art Deco style. The town centre is worth a visit, boasting Australia's largest concentration of

Art Deco buildings, with examples of Spanish, Sicilian, Moroccan, Italian and Anglo Saxon Art Deco design facades.

Canecutter Way is a major highlight of this region and is a 52km scenic drive between Kurrimine Beach and Innisfail. It is billed as the 'Greatest Detour in North Queensland'.

It offers plenty of reasons to leave the Bruce Highway to catch a glimpse of the sweet life in the tropics. Named for the men who cut the sugar cane by hand with cane knives in the days before mechanised harvesters, the Canecutter Way meanders from the Coral Sea-lapped shores of laid-back Kurrimine Beach, past cane land and papaya and banana plantations, through picturesque towns with old country pubs and World Heritage-listed rainforest to Innisfail and the southern access to the Atherton Tablelands via the Palmerston Highway.

ATTRACTIONS Kurrimine Beach is famous for King Reef, which is so close to shore that walking tours are offered on the lowest of low tides. It is also popular with fisher folk.

A leading attraction nearby is the Berryman family's Murdering Point Winery, where visitors can enjoy free guided tropical fruit wine tasting and discussion of the bush tucker and locally sourced fruits used to make the medal-winning wine. Quality dry, sweet and fortified wines are produced from fruits such as mango, passionfruit and lychee and bush tucker like Lemon Aspen.

Follow the road to Silkwood, which maintains religious and cultural immigrant links with Italy. The tradition of the Feast of the Three Saints is celebrated on the first Sunday of May, with a parade, feast and fireworks. The town is home to Aussie Pepper and the smallest National Australia Bank building (no longer a bank).

Mena Creek's history is flavoured with the romantic story of Jose Paronella, a Spanish immigrant with a dream and a passion for castles and hard work. In the 1930s he opened his pleasure gardens and reception centre, Paronella Park, powering the venture with hydroelectric generators. Today the dream continues at this restored, intriguing venue. During the day, visitors are charmed by guided tours, including the Tunnel of

Love. By night, the park presents a dramatic evening tour.

Paronella Park was voted the number one thing to do in the 2009 RACQ poll and has since been recognised as the best major tourism attraction in the region. Camping and cabin accommodation is available.

Visitors can also stay locally at the caravan park and camping grounds with its six boutique cabins or at the Mena Creek Hotel, which offers air-conditioned rooms (including family room options).

Mena Creek is home to a number of walks, including the Gorrell Track, an easy 3.7km to MacNamee Creek's lush rainforest and picnic spot. The cane train track runs through the centre of South Johnstone so it is a good place to grab a coffee or a beer and experience the sight of the colourful little locomotives hauling cane bins to the local mill during the sugar cane crushing season.

Next stop is Wangan where award- winning pies are on offer.

The southern access to the Atherton Tablelands provides a scenic drive along the 55km Palmerston Highway from the coast, through Wooroonooran National Park, to the township of Millaa Millaa at the top of the range. After turning off the Bruce Highway 5km north of Innisfail, the vista opens out on to cattle and cane farm land with breathtaking views of mountain fringed valleys and the southern aspect of Mt Bartle Frere.

At 1622m, this is Queensland's highest mountain. Continue past the Nucifora tea plantation and into the World Heritage rainforest, stopping en route to experience the Mamu Tropical Skywalk, a 350m elevated walkway

in the traditional country of the Mamu Aboriginal people. It offers close-up views of rainforest plants, insects and birds high up in the rainforest canopy, along with spectacular panoramic views of the World Heritage Area, including North Johnstone River gorge and surrounding rainforest-clad peaks.

There are numerous camping areas and places to swim in the cool, fresh water of the North Johstone River

as you drive through Wooroonooran National Park. Sections of the Palmerston Highway are quite steep so observe the speed limits. Keep an eye out for the overhead "possum ladders", which allow native animals to cross from rainforest on one side of the wide road to the other without having to come to the ground and risk being hit by vehicles. The endangered Southern Cassowary and even feral pigs (definitely ground-dwellers) have been spotted along this section of highway.

From Millaa Millaa continue on the Millaa-Malanda road or take the Old Palmerston Highway tourist drive (not suitable for caravans) to the Kennedy Highway north of Ravenshoe.

Food and Drink

Your Guide to Atherton Tablelands' Wineries

Dotted around the Atherton Tablelands are wineries and distilleries to discover and relish at your leisure

Meet your new favourite Uncle

Mount Uncle Distillery at Walkamin has an excellent reputation for world class spirits and liqueurs and is run by the same people who founded it 18 years ago. Gins, rums, whiskies and liqueurs many made with locally grown fruit are produced on site at this craft distillery.

Drop by for a drop of the good stuff the cellar door is open seven days from 10am to 4pm though call ahead just to be sure. Highlights include Helga the 1500 litre copper pot quite a gal and the barrel room with more than 200 barrels. Built on a piece of paradise, the lovely grounds include a banana plantation and friendly alpacas, donkeys, goats and peacocks who call Mount Uncle Distillery home. Roam around the parklands, enjoy a tasting with knowledgeable staff and have a peek at how things are done in a boutique distillery with a giant reputation.

Mt Uncle Distillery is signposted from Chewko Rd, 15.5km south of Mareeba

Fruitful visit to boutique winery
De Brueys Boutique Wines blends tradition and innovation to make wines, ports and liqueurs from a diversity of fruits, including lychee, mango, jaboticaba, bush cherry, mulberry, passionfruit and

star apple. It has won numerous awards at the Australian Fruit Wine Awards including the top gong for liqueurs with its Flagship Coffee Elixir.

De Brueys started life as a mango farm and has developed into a trailblazer for fine fruit wines.

This winemaker is full of surprises: a nice dry red wine made from jaboticaba fruit or a tasty port from mulberries anyone? There's a cellar door for tastings and attention has been lavished on the grounds, including preserving the natural setting, which includes kangaroos, wallabies, possums, quolls bandicoots and birdlife plus freshwater crocodiles in the creek at the rear of the property.

De Brueys makes the most of Tropical North Queensland's natural assets and wants to share the riches with visitors.

De Brueys Boutique Wines is on Fichera Rd, 2km off the Kennedy Highway off Tinaroo Creek Rd.

A drop of the good stuff

Golden Drop Winery as its name suggests makes luscious wines from mangos. This mango farm turns its distinctive fruit into wines, ports and liqueurs such as cellos. Visitors can sample the fermented product but also take a tour of a working mango orchard and in season, buy some of the golden harvest on the spot.

Golden Drop is a family run business and it took the Nastasi family a great deal of research and development along with blood, sweat and tears to make their first dry, medium and sweet mango wines in 1999. The process is quite different from grape wines and their dedication shows in all their products. A visit to Golden Drop is more than just a wine tasting, it's a chance to visit one of Australia's largest mango farms, savour the immaculate surroundings and talk to friendly people passionate about the glory of fruit wines.

*Golden Drop Winery is at Biboohra, 10 minutes from Mareeba. Turn right off the highway and follow the signs for 2kms

Experience the Atherton Tablelands Craft Distilleries and Wineries

We may be a little too warm for traditional grape growing but that hasn't stopped an innovative and pioneering band of artisans making a huge range of wines, spirits and liqueurs on the Atherton Tablelands. Tasting anything from a mango wine to a citrus cello or a coffee liqueur makes a cellar door visit here a happy adventure for your taste buds.

Mt Uncle

Surrounded by cane fields, it's not surprising Mt Uncle Distillery produces award winning rum but it also makes gin, whiskey and vodka. There's also a cheeky little marshmallow liqueur called SexyCat in its repertoire.

Formed in 2001 at Walkamin by head distiller and director Mark Watkins, Mt Uncle champions local and nationally sourced ingredients.

It has its own volcanic spring water source. Known as North Queensland's first and only distillery, the cellar door is open 10am to 4pm. Bridges Bar and Restaurant is also on the property along with lush grounds to roam, which include a banana farm.

Golden Drop

Mango wine is not easy to make but the Nastasi family of Mareeba have cracked it. A former tobacco farm, the Nastasi's developed a successful 17,500 tree Australian Kensington Red Mango plantation on their land but wanted to diversify.

After much research and hard yakka, the Golden Drop Winery opened in 1999 with the world's first commercial mango wine.

Their initial offering from the Biboohra property was dry, medium and sweet varieties but now as well as mango wines they make port liqueurs and citrus cellos. Their cellar door is open 9am to 5.30pm and visitors can see where their purchases came from with a look at a working plantation.

Murdering Point Winery

If it's grown locally it's a good bet Murdering Point Winerycan turn it into wine.

The Silkwood winery produce red and white wines, ports, liqueurs and creams made from typical tropical fruits such as mango, lychee and pineapple through to more exotic varieties Davidson plum, black sapote, vanilla and jaboticaba the Brazilian native which grows sweet black fruit on its trunk.

Founded by the Berryman family in 2001, Murdering Point Winery has won numerous Australian Fruit Wine Show champion and gold awards, especially for their Panama Gold made from mangoes and aged in French oak barrels. The cellar door is open 9.30 to 5pm.

de Brueys

de Brueys original founders Bob and Elaine de Bruey named their Mareeba winery after an ancestor who was a valiant vice-admiral on one of Napoleon's ships in the battle of the Nile.

Their own story has a better ending with the couple now retired having sold their winery to Double Island Resort owner Benny Wu. de Brueys passionfruit wine has won a best dry wine championship at the Australian Fruit Wine Awards and their Flagship Coffee Liqueur has been named best liqueur.

The raw materials for their winery, sugar cane and tropical fruits, come from either the farm or neighbouring properties. The wines are produced up to 12 months before sale and adhere to wine industry standards for clarity and stability. It's a working commercial winery with a special viewing platform for visitors. The cellar door is open 10am to 5pm.

Rainforest Heart

Deep in Mungalli bush land Rainforest Heart transforms native fruit into wine. It's latest Davidson's Plum Royale, a fortified native fruit wine aperitif. They also make fruit spritzers from the bush tucker grown on the 400 plus hectare property on the edge of Wooroonooran National Park.

Founded and managed by Margo Watkins and her partner Peter, Rainforest Heart offers personalised tours of this unique orchard and farm, near Millaa Millaa. The cellar door is by appointment only.

5 Cute and Quirky Eats on the Atherton Tablelands

Petals and Pinecones
The life mission of Petals and Pinecones is to have you leave just that little bit happier. And this one-of-a-kind café can't miss. It's a glorious blend of the healthy think smoothie bowls to the most pumped up, blinged out milkshakes you'll ever see. The Atherton café has generously sized dishes that look like a work of art and use heaps of fresh fruit and vegetables. Tucked away behind the SuperCheap Auto carpark, it caters for everyone including vegans and has brilliant coffee to boot. Family owned, this uplifting, fun café experience will have you buzzing.

Nick's Restaurant

Nick's Restaurant in Yungaburra is part Swiss diner, part alpine lodge and part community meeting place. It's vibrant, welcoming and the food is delicious. In a world of nondescript restaurants, going to Nick's is actually going somewhere. There are skis and a herb garden at the front door and in this big, busy restaurant diners are happy and often noisy. With a mix of Swiss and Italian cuisine there's plenty of pasta, pizza, antipasto platters and Swiss treats such as rosti, bratwurst and Kaseschnitte, which is wine and cheese on toast. Honestly. Service is fun and friendly, and on an exceptional night there could be music and singing.

Tin Town Sweets

Lolly shops are heaven: jars and jars of sweet jewels covering the shelves as far as they eye can see. And they're equally tempting when you're all grown up. Think bullseyes, milk bottles, sherbet lemons, humbugs, acid drops, gumballs and other old-time delights. Tin Town Sweets in Herberton is a happy place of lollies, chocolate and liquorice by the scoop, with a café for good measure.

Frogs

This café in the jungle has kangaroo, emu and crocodile on the menu and real water dragons running round the deck. There's large murals of rainforest animals on the walls but sit outside this Kuranda institution and the flora and fauna are real. Frogs was established in 1980 by Terry Pates and he still runs it along with his wife Victoria. Customers love the single origin coffee and the barramundi caught just down the road. There's also a good range of curries and homemade goodies such as macadamia, tomato and smoked chilli sauce. The laid-back vibe, free wi-fi and super service make locals and visitors love Frogs.

Coffee Works

Described as Disneyland for coffee, Coffee Works in Mareeba is a café and museum where entry buys you all day tastings of incredible edibles including coffee, tea, chocolate and liqueur in unlimited quantities. It's also a fabulous collection of tea and coffee artefacts and collectables dating back as far as the 1700s. Consider it a treasure chest for the tastebuds. Chocolates are made on the premises and there's also small batch roasting of a huge range of beans sourced globally. If you counted the varieties you'd get past 40. The Mareeba premises and other locations round Tropical North Queensland grew from a single stall at Rusty's Markets in Cairns in 1988 and founders Annie and Rob Webber are acknowledged pioneers of Australia's coffee culture.

Yungaburra Christmas Markets
Still looking for Christmas gifts?

Have a stroll through the Yungaburra Christmas Market and you might be able to tick off that box!

The Yungaburra Market is the biggest and oldest market on the Atherton Tablelands. Local producers gather on the commons in the middle of the historic village of Yungaburra to sell fresh produce, flowers, home made crafts, local wines, wooden furniture, clothing and just about anything else you can think of.

Time & Date for 2017: December 17 2017, from 7.30am to 12.30pm
Location: Bruce Jones Park, Yungaburra

The Atherton Tablelands On a Plate

Fresh local produce, unique food experiences and some of the region's favourite chefs will be celebrated as the Atherton Tablelands' most exciting culinary event returns in October 2017.

With a new expanded format, Tastes of the Tablelands will be held on Saturday evening, October 14 and all day Sunday, October 15 at the Hou Wang Temple, Atherton.

The Rotary Club of Atherton, which celebrates its 70-year anniversary this year, are once again hosting this much-anticipated regional foodie day out.

Tastes of the Tablelands event manager Kirsty Densmore has promised a dynamic weekend filled with inspirational food, and fun cooking demonstrations.

"It's a real celebration of local culinary diversity", Ms Densmore said. "We want to inspire people to cook innovatively and passionately learning from the region's most most talented foodies, producers and providores."

Seating under shady canopies will provide the perfect vantage point for the various cooking competitions, demonstrations and entertainment that will be held on the new cookery stage.

Assorted artists and children's entertainment will also fill the grounds of the old temple, a link to the Tablelands' Chinese past, with live music from some of Yungaburra Folk Festival's headline acts including Jango in the Jungle and perennial favourites Swamp Dogs.

New events this year include a barbecue competition, showcasing high quality sustainable raised meat, while the new dedicated cooking stage will offer fast moving, high energy food-related demonstrations and mystery box competitions.

The local celebrity cook off will be what, Ms Densmore describes, as a real spectator sport, open to all sorts of "bribery, corruption and blackmail". Sustainability workshops will round out the program of events.

Ms Densmore said the five-course dinner will also see producers and chefs from across the region work together to offer a five-course locally-sourced but internationally inspired menu on the night.

These include Mungalli Creek Dairy, Smokin' Hot Q, Little Red Hen Catering, Jet Soul Food, Gallo Dairy and Tableland Wagyu Beef.

"We want people to come along for the entire weekend, spending the night in Atherton, taking in the atmosphere of the event, appreciating the food and ultimately having a great time," she said.

Michael Trout, chair of Tropical Tablelands Tourism (TTT), said the popularity of Tastes of the Tablelands continued to grow each year and the expanded format would ultimately encourage people to stay in the destination longer.

"More and more people are seeking holiday destinations that combine natural beauty with fresh, delicious produce and a wide range of accommodation to suit various tastes and budgets," he said.

Taste of the Tablelands will be held in the grounds of Hou Wang Temple, Herberton Road, Atherton, from October 14-15.

The dinner is priced at $70 per person. Entry costs for the Sunday are: $10. Those under 12 admitted free.

The End

www.ingramcontent.com/pod-product-compliance
Lightning Source LLC
Chambersburg PA
CBHW030000110526
44587CB00011BA/925